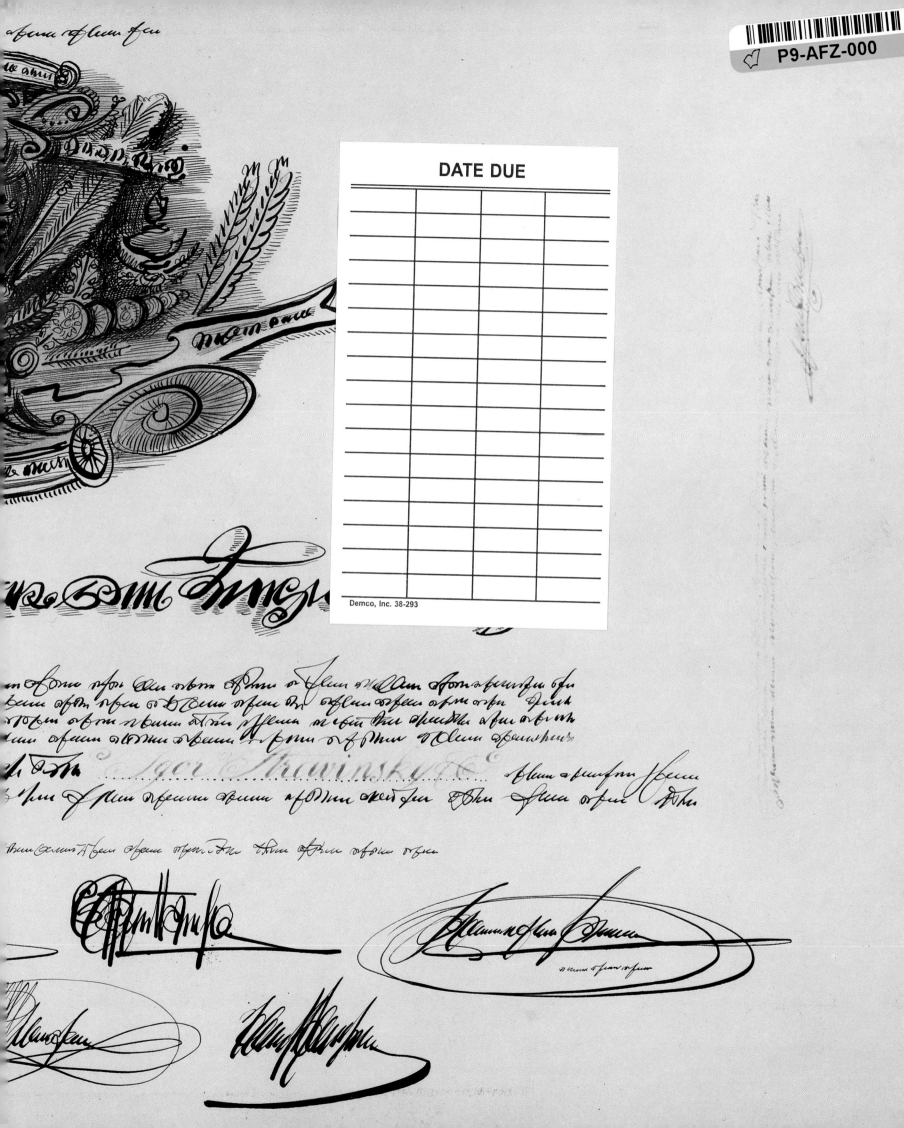

Robert Craft

A Stravinsky Scrapbook
1940~1971

Illustrations chosen by Patricia Schwark

Thames and Hudson

Riverside Community College
'12 Library
4800 Magnolia Avenue
Riverside, CA 92506

ML88.S86 S8 1983
A Stravinsky scrapbook,
1940-1971

Endpapers: Mock Diploma for Igor Stravinsky
& Co. by Saul Steinberg, 1950.

Any copy of this book issued by the publisher
as a paperback is sold subject to the condition
that it shall not, by way of trade or otherwise,
be lent, resold, hired out or otherwise
circulated without the publisher's prior
consent in any form of binding or cover other
than that in which it is published, and without
a similar condition including these words
being imposed on a subsequent purchaser.

Designed by Sue Ebrahim

© 1983 Robert Craft

First published in the USA in 1983 by Thames
and Hudson Inc., 500 Fifth Avenue, New York,
New York 10110

Library of Congress Catalog Card Number
83-50016

All Rights Reserved. No part of this
publication may be reproduced or transmitted
in any form or by any means, electronic or
mechanical, including photocopy, recording
or any other information storage and retrieval
system, without permission in writing from the
publisher.

Printed and bound in Great Britain.

Foreword

Whereas *Igor and Vera Stravinsky* (Thames and Hudson, 1982) honored a fifty-year love affair, the present book focuses on the composer's musical life, presenting facsimiles of some of his completed manuscripts, sketches, and notational jottings, as well as views of him at the piano, conducting, and listening—at rehearsals, recording sessions, and as part of the audience. The book contains a number of sections in which the material is devoted to a single composition and the circumstances of its performance, from *Orpheus*—when I first appeared on the scene—through *The Rake's Progress*, the Shakespeare Songs, the Septet, the *Canticum Sacrum*, *Agon*, *Threni*, Movements, *A Sermon, a Narrative, and a Prayer*, *The Flood*, *Abraham and Isaac*, and the *Requiem Canticles*.

Unlike the earlier volume, this one does not feature Stravinsky in company with other celebrities, and the pictures of him on his travels are largely of the performing artist en route to his concert engagements. Other aspects of Stravinsky's work are also shown: his calculations of expenses, replies to questionnaires, and memos for program notes. There are also doodles confirming what we already know—that he was original in everything he did.

More important even than the pictorial record of Stravinsky's final thirty years are his medical diaries, since these were written as reminders and intended only for his own eyes and those of doctors and tax accountants (see the Appendix). For a man who was seriously ill during most of the period of the book, almost all of the pictures reveal him in a remarkably happy mood, while the others, so far from being studies in melancholy, are of a man deep in concentration.

Of the many turning points in Stravinsky's life, perhaps the most important are the beginning of his work with Rimsky-Korsakov, the discovery by Diaghilev and the commissioning of *Firebird*, the estrangement from Russia in 1917, the meeting with Vera Sudeikina in 1921, and the move to the United States in 1939. Hollywood differed more radically from anywhere in Europe than did Berlin, Paris, and Vienna from Stravinsky's native St. Petersburg. These last years—the so-called American period—and particularly the 1940s and 1950s, remain the least known and least documented of his mature life, less than his preceding nineteen years' residence in France, or, until now, the first eighteen years in Russia—for, after June 1910, he spent only ten months in his native country.

In the early 1940s, Stravinsky's concertizing and traveling were curtailed by the war, and the photographic record is correspondingly slender. *The Rake's Progress* changed this, partly for the reason that it brought Stravinsky back to

Europe and placed him in direct communication with its musical and artistic life. (The reactionary American political scene of 1951 and the rebirth of Europe might well have made his visit permanent.) In any case, his vistas broadened, and invitations to conduct in Europe and to fulfill commissions from there were in contrast to American neglect. To the end of his life and after, he was more widely acclaimed abroad than in his adopted country. Consider that in the 1950s he was still conducting second-rate American orchestras, and that his programs were only half made up of his own music, while in Europe whole festivals were centered on him and his work.

1956/1957 was the crucial year. In October 1956, Stravinsky was felled by a stroke that placed his life in jeopardy, and for the remaining fifteen years he was never free from serious illness. This occupied far more of his time, and bore more heavily upon him, than he ever revealed. In June 1957, on the occasion of his 75th birthday, he unveiled a new work, *Agon*, that was to add further distinction to his now unchallenged sovereignity as the greatest living composer; and from then until the end of his life, his position as one of the handful of truly great artists of the twentieth century never ceased to grow.

From this date, too, films and photographic material increase in proportion. Few airport arrivals and departures went unrecorded, and Stravinsky became a public figure, apparently bearing little relation to the semi-reclusive composer whom I had known in 1948 in the cottage in the Hollywood hills, a man whose main recreations were going to the movies two or three times a week, taking drives to ocean and desert, and listening to music at small, local concerts or on records.

It may seem curious, therefore, that in a book covering the American years, more than half of these photographs were taken abroad, and, of those, a third again in Venice. But, surely, everyone takes more snapshots in foreign places than in his living room.

I do not apologize for my prominence in this book. I was there, I lived and worked with Stravinsky, and to have cropped myself from all of the pictures in which I appear would have distorted the truth. Besides, when Stravinsky's correspondence of the period is finally published, my role will be seen to have been far greater than the one presented here photographically. Nor do I apologize for the matter-of-factness of the text: the necessity for compression in the captions did not permit indulgence in concinnities.

2 *1949*. Igor by Vera.

3 *1949*. Vera by Igor.

4 *December 1939.* Hollywood. Walt Disney's cartoon of Stravinsky. The composer went from Hollywood to Dumbarton Oaks for the New Year, then to New York for concerts with the Philharmonic. On January 11, 1940, Vera Sudeikina arrived in New York. A few days later, Stravinsky and his fiancée went to Pittsburgh, where he fulfilled conducting engagements.

4

Drops Incognito

IGOR STRAVINSKY
Arriving here two weeks before his scheduled guest appearances as conductor with the Pittsburgh Symphony Orchestra, Mr. Stravinsky originally meant to remain incognito, found he couldn't—and finally held a press conference.

5

5 *January 17, 1940.* Pittsburgh. Newspaper photograph. Stravinsky, Mme Sudeikina, and the composer's secretary, Alexis Kall, arrived in Pittsburgh (Hotel Webster Hall) on January 15, though the composer's concerts with the local orchestra (*Apollo, Petrushka, Jeu de cartes, Firebird* suite) did not take place until January 26 and 28. "I came here, instead of remaining in New York," he said in an interview, "to work on my fourth symphony. It is quieter here." (He also said that what he liked best in America—"my two loves"—are "baked potatoes and drug stores.") At a reception after the concert of the 26th, he read a speech: "I am very touched that you all wanted to spend with me this evening after my first appearance as a conductor in your great city. [Stravinsky and Samuel Dushkin had given a recital in Pittsburgh on January 25, 1935.] I use this opportunity to tell you how happy you made me by giving me the possibility of making the Pittsburgh audience acquainted with different epochs of my music. The magnificent apparatus that I used—your wonderful symphony orchestra that under the expert hands of Fritz Reiner and his talented colleague Vladimir Bakaleinikoff became a solid ensemble—gave me a real artistic delight, and you see before you a happy man. In conclusion I want to say (what should be repeated everywhere) that nowhere in the world a musical activity of such magnitude can be seen as [in] the U.S.A. I thank you." On February 2, the threesome returned to New York. Mme Sudeikina went from there to Charleston, S.C., to spend a month with friends. Stravinsky and Kall returned to Boston.

1st Marriage:
Serge Soudeikine
Date Febr 11, 1918
Yalta, Crimea
U.S.F.S.R.

Date and place marri-
-age terminated
Febr 20, 1920 Tiflis,
Republic of Georgia
Caucasus
manner of termination
of such marriage:
DIVORSE

6

6 On March 4, 1940, in Bedford, Massachusetts, Igor and Vera filed "notice of their Intention of Marriage." Since the bride was unable to furnish a certified copy of her divorce decree, Arthur E. Carson, the assistant Town Clerk of Bedford, wrote to Probate Judge Arthur E. Beane, of Cambridge, Mass., asking him to grant the certificate, "if satisfied of the truth of the statements made to him." Stravinsky forthwith invented marriage and divorce dates and places for Mme Sudeikina, the certificate was granted, and the civil ceremony took place, in Bedford, on March 9. The marriage was performed by Carson, and the witnesses were Dr. Alexis Kall and Dr. Timothy Taracuzio.

7 *May 1940*. Gerry's Landing, Cambridge, Mass. The newly-wed Stravinskys, the Edward Forbes family, and Dr. Alexis Kall (with cigar; Stravinsky's Russian translator).

7

8

10

9

11

12

8–12 In July 1940, Stravinsky conducted the Mexico City Symphony in concerts and recordings, after which he and his wife re-entered the United States from Mexico as Russian non-quota immigrants. Back in Los Angeles, they immediately applied for American citizenship. (**10**) *September 1940.* At the San Francisco World's Fair. (**11**) With Carlos Chavez. (The other photographs were taken in Mexico.)

13 *September 1940.* Los Gatos. With Adolph and Beata Bolm.

13

Friday, December 20, 1946

Composer's Wife Rushes to Finish Yule Shopping

MRS. IGOR STRAVINSKY
"So many lovely things in your shops"

14

Minneapolis Equals Paris in Merchandise, She Claims

By DOROTHY RILEY
Star Journal Staff Writer

Even as you and I, Mrs. Igor Stravinsky is frantically doing her last minute Christmas shopping.

She is the wife of the modernist composer who is to be guest conductor of the Minneapolis Symphony orchestra at Friday night's concert.

The conductor and his wife will be in New York for Christmas.

Married a little over a year ago in Boston the Stravinskys, after the present tour, will head for California where they expect to set up housekeeping.

Mrs. Stravinsky, before her marriage, was the well known interior decorator, Vera Bossert and already has definite plans about the house.

"It will be a rambling one story building," she said. "There will be plenty of grounds as we both want chickens, dogs, cats and maybe a cow."

Not only will they be building a home but they will be starting life as many other Americans, for by then they hope to be citizens of the United States. Both have made application for citizenship.

* * *

* * *

Minneapolis weather is well suited to Mrs. Stravinsky's taste as she was born in Russia. HER ONLY COMPLAINT IS THAT IT IS NOT COLD ENOUGH.

Mrs. Stravinsky likes traveling and acts as her husband's secretary. Just as any other wife, when she feels her husband is concentrating too deeply on his work she does something about it.

In her own room Mrs. Stravinsky is going to cover one of the walls in white silk on which she will draw a map of her beloved Paris.

The Star Spangled Banner

Harmonized and arranged for male chorus by Igor Stravinsky, 1941

Copyright by Igor Stravinsky 1941

17

18

16–19 *The Star-Spangled Banner.* (**16**, **17**) The composer never heard his beautiful male-chorus arrangement of the national anthem, so much richer harmonically than his published version of the piece. (**18**) Stravinsky's frame around the title is red, white, and blue in the original. (**19**) The first-violin part is Stravinsky's copy, used by him the first time he conducted the piece, August 27, 1940.

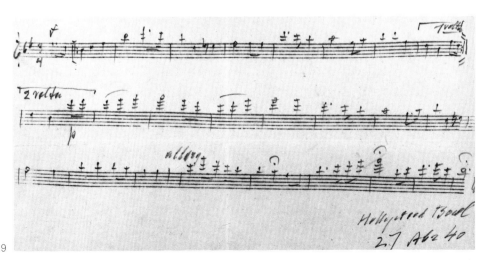

19

20 *1942.* Hollywood. With Oscar Levant.

21 *September 1944.* 1260 North Wetherly Drive, Hollywood. With Nadia Boulanger.

22 *1945.* Los Angeles.

23 *1943.* 1260 North Wetherly Drive. Stravinsky holds a bag of his chickens as he prepares to give them away after protests from neighbors.

24 *1944.* Santa Barbara. Vera in a hammock.

25 *1946.* In Santa Barbara.

22

23

24

25

28

26, 27 *1945*. The Stravinskys' Certificates of Naturalization.

28 *1947*. Vera Stravinsky's passport photo.

29, 30 *December 1946*. New York. With Vittorio ("Totor") Rieti. Photo by Henri Cartier-Bresson. The 12-tone greeting ("From Igor season greetings to Totor") dates from the 1960s.

29

30 ....

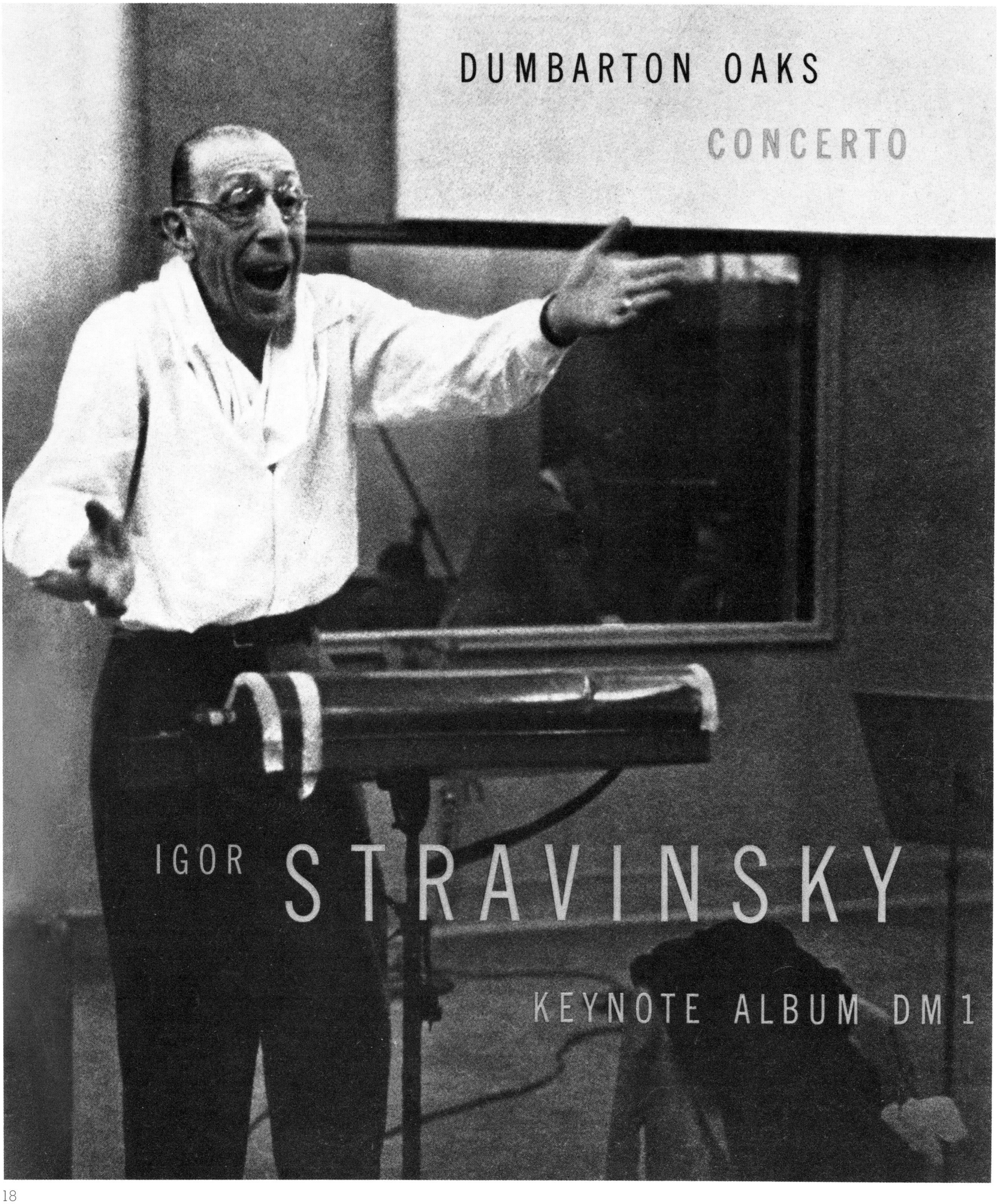

DUMBARTON OAKS
CONCERTO

IGOR STRAVINSKY

KEYNOTE ALBUM DM 1

31

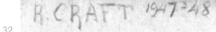

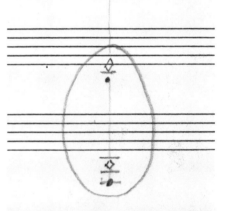

31 *April 1947.* New York. Recording the *Dumbarton Oaks* Concerto. Photograph by Fred Plaut. Mrs. Stravinsky and Alexis Haieff are visible in the control room.

32 *August 1946.* Robert Craft at Tanglewood.

33 *Spring 1946.* 1260 North Wetherly Drive.

34 Chord from the Spring Concerto arranged for five instruments.

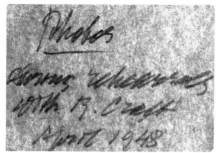

37

38

39

40

41

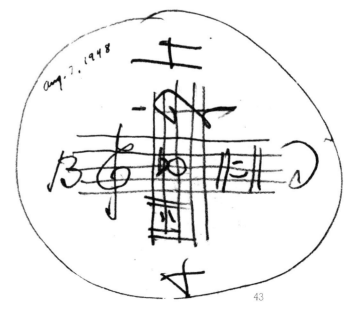

42

43

S. KOUSSEVITZKY

Night Letter

Your orchestra is wonderful
~~incomparably~~
Your ~~wonderful~~ orchestra gave me great
pleasure and we achieved a huge success,
unfortunately the twenty-five years of your
brilliant influence taught the press nothing.
It remained provincial and hostile. It would be
delightful to see you, at Ambassador N.Y.
until the 28. Affectionately.

49

44

45

46

38, 39, 41 *April 10, 1948.* New York. With Alexis Haieff.

43 *August 7, 1948.* Stravinsky's spelling of "Bach" in clefs drawn on a napkin in a Hollywood restaurant.

44 *March 14, 1949.* On February 6, 1949, I accompanied the Stravinskys to Boston, where he conducted the Boston Symphony in Cambridge on the 10th, in Boston on the 11th and 12th. Receiving the usual negative reviews, he asked me to draft a telegram praising Kussevitzky and, at the same time, condemning the Boston critics. The result, written on our return to New York (Ambassador Hotel, February 13) and the first of many collaborative efforts by Mr. and Mrs. Stravinsky and myself, typifies our personalities: generous words in large letters by Mrs. Stravinsky, crabbed text (and handwriting) by myself, precision (the date) by Stravinsky. While in Boston, Stravinsky suffered an attack of food poisoning. Max Rinkel, the doctor who treated him, became a permanent member of the Stravinsky East Coast entourage.

45 *July 31, 1948.* 1260 North Wetherly Drive.

46 *July 1949.* 1260 North Wetherly Drive. Photograph by Stravinsky.

To Bob (Robert Craft)
cordially IStr Hollywood/48

49

47 *February 1949.* New York. Manhattan Center (34th Street). Recording Orpheus.

48 Sketch for *Orpheus.*

49, 50 *February 1949.* New York. Manhattan Center. Recording *Orpheus.* (50) With George Balanchine.

50

51

53 *September 4, 1949.* A *corrida* in Tijuana. On September 2, the Stravinskys and I drove to San Diego (Grant Hotel). The weekend was the emotional climax of the summer for me. I had planned to return to New York by bus on September 5, but I had become so attached to the Stravinskys that I was already homesick at the prospect of even a short separation. On the morning of the 4th, Eugene Berman and Ona Munson joined us at La Jolla for a drive to Ensenada (Baja California). At the *corrida*, Stravinsky showed great enthusiasm for the pageantry and the music, and, unlike his wife, did not avert his eyes from the slaughter. We returned to Los Angeles in silence and, at six o'clock the next morning, she drove me, lump in my throat, to the Greyhound Bus Terminal. I felt so miserable when she had left me, however, that I reclaimed my bag and caught up with her in a taxi half-way back to Wetherly Drive. Not until the next evening did I find the courage to leave, this time by plane. I returned to California in October, again in November, and in December permanently.

51 *1949.* Hollywood. The staircase leads to the gardens behind the Stravinsky home.

52 *September 1949.* 1260 North Wetherly Drive.

EL TOREO DE

TIJUANA, B. C.

IMP. ABOITIZ - MEX.

N.º 130

BARRERA 3a. FILA

SOL

RINGSIDE 3rd. ROW
SUNNY SIDE

ENTRADA A LA LOCALIDAD

Before its performance in Town Hall on Oct. 21, Erika von Wagner rehearses the Sprechstimme of Arnold Schönberg's Pierrot Lunaire with Robert Craft conducting members of the Chamber Art Society. Drawing by B. F. Dolbin

54

54 *October 21, 1950*. The pianist is Edward Steuermann, the violinist Isadore Cohen, and the cellist Seymour Barab.

55 *May 1950*. Near Rapid City, South Dakota, after driving from Pierre through the Badlands. On our transcontinental automobile trips, Stravinsky insisted on stopping at roadside exhibits advertising desert reptiles and "monsters."

56 *March 1951*. In the living room of 1260 North Wetherly Drive. Two summers later, the window in the left corner of the picture was to become part of the wall of an enlarged dining room, the "Dylan Thomas den."

55

56

57

59

58

Perséphone

To Bob
(Robert Craft)
with much love
I St
7/2/51

60

57, 58 *July 1951*. At the Huxleys'. Seated at the table are Grace and Edwin Hubble, and Maria Huxley.

59 *February 28, 1951*. Havana. With Margarita Montero (harpist) and Gustavo Pittaluga (Spanish composer and friend). This *El Mundo* photograph was taken on the arrival of the Stravinskys by air from Miami. They had left Los Angeles by automobile on February 20, spent the night at Wickenburg (Arizona), the ones after that at El Paso, Breckenridge (Texas), Shreveport (where Stravinsky learned of the death of André Gide), Mobile, and St. Augustine. After two days at Pompano Beach, the Stravinskys drove to Miami, left

their car in a garage, took a taxi to the airport, and flew in a Cuban plane to Havana (El Presidente Hotel). That evening, Pittaluga took them to dinner at the Zaragozana and to a guitar-orchestra concert. On March 1, 2, and 3, Stravinsky rehearsed the Filarmonica for his two concerts, Sunday morning, March 4, and Monday night, March 5 (*Ode*, *Scènes de Ballet*, the Two Little Suites, String Concerto, Divertimento). Between these appearances, the Stravinskys visited the studio of the painter Wilfredo Lam.

Stravinsky had conducted in Havana on March 3 and 4, 1946, having traveled by train from Boston to Miami, and from there by airplane. At that time, the composer and his

wife spent two nights at the Tarafa sugar plantation, to which they journeyed from Havana on a private train. The Stravinskys later told how their hostess assured them that, in case of difficulty in sleeping, they should ring for coffee. Stravinsky's 1946 program consisted of the Overture to *Ruslan*, Tchaikovsky's Second Symphony, *Scènes de Ballet*, and the 1945 *Firebird* Suite. They flew to Miami on March 5 and went to Dallas, by train through Jacksonville and New Orleans, for more concerts.

61 *1949. The Rake's Progress*. First draft of the full score, Act I, scene 2.

26

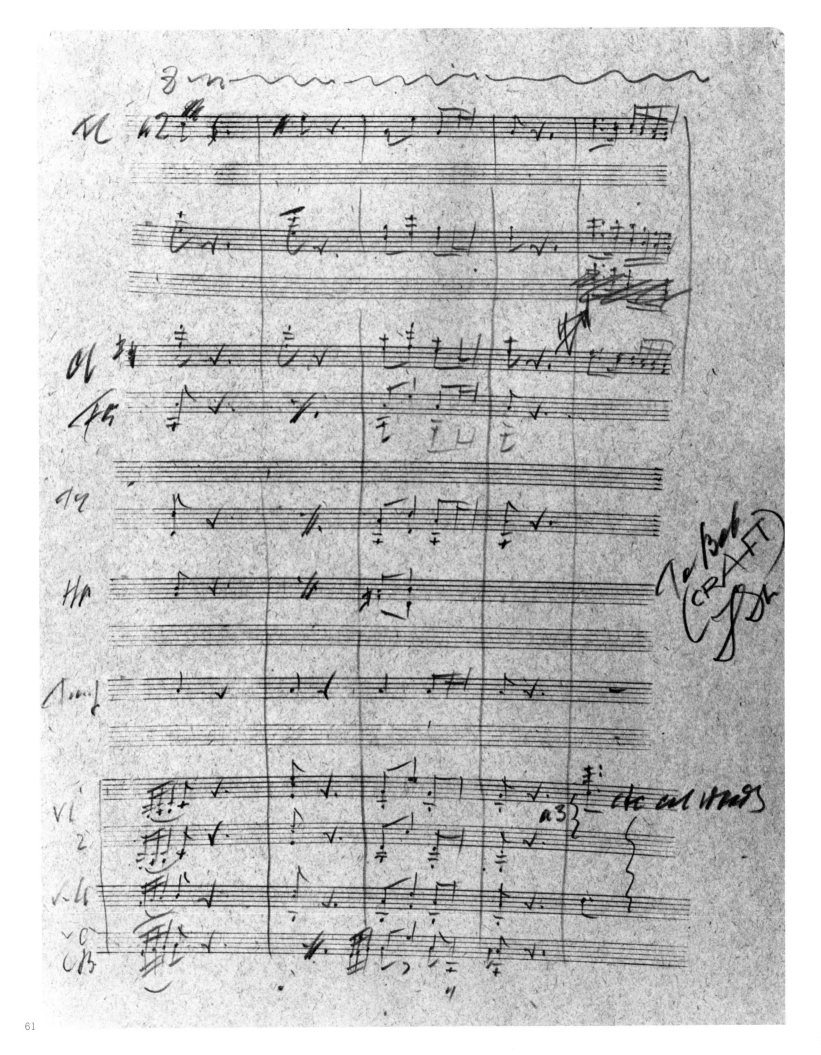

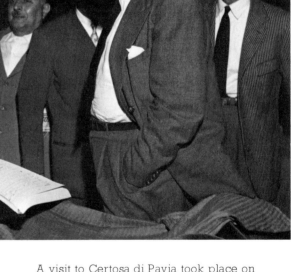

62 *August 26, 1951.* Arriving at Milan railroad station. The Stravinskys had left Naples for Milan on the 10:40 a.m. rapido, and arrived at 9 p.m. (Hotel Duomo, where a nurse awaited the composer to give him an injection of penicillin, since he was not fully recovered from the pneumonia that had detained him for ten days in Naples). The Milan railroad station was crowded with journalists, and photographs of the Stravinskys, similar to the one in *Oggi*, appeared in other magazines and newspapers as well. In the morning of August 27, the Stravinskys walked to the Sforzesco. In the evening, they were at La

Scala for the first rehearsal of *The Rake's Progress*. (Auden and Kallman arrived from their Naples train about an hour later.) On August 28, the Stravinskys attended a 10 a.m. rehearsal, spent the afternoon in the Brera, and were at La Scala in the evening. Rehearsals filled the 29th and 30th. On the 31st, the Stravinskys visited Santa Maria delle Grazie and the Ambrosiana, and on September 1, Sant'Ambrogio. On September 2, they were in Bellagio for lunch, spent the afternoon in Bergamo, and, back in Milan, dined with Auden and Kallman, going with them afterwards to a performance of *Fedora*.

A visit to Certosa di Pavia took place on September 4, but the Stravinskys returned to Milan in time to attend a cocktail party given by Auden.

63 *August 27, 1951.* La Scala, Milan. The first rehearsal of *The Rake's Progress*.

64, 65 *September 3, 1951.* Milan. Rehearsals at La Scala for *The Rake's Progress.* (65) The short man in the center is Carlo Corbellini, the composer's physician. To his left are Carl Ebert, the stage director, and Gianni Ratto, the scenery and costume designer.

66

68, 69 *September 11, 1951*. Teatro La Fenice, Venice. (**68**) During the intermission. (**69**) Curtain call for the composer and Elisabeth Schwarzkopf (Anne), Nell Tangeman (Mother Goose), Auden, and Kallman.

Eugenio Montale wrote in his diary: "Venice, September 8, 1951, . . . Lord knows whether I will succeed in getting a close look at Stravinsky. . . . The Maestro, it appears, is rather acid, *arancino* as they say in Florence, with journalists. . . . September 8, evening. I succeeded in getting hold of the libretto of *The Rake's Progress*, which is a jewel of its kind and contains possibly the loveliest verses Auden ever wrote. . . . But this is not as functional a libretto as Auden perhaps believes. What music could underline verses that jump from the style of Sullivan's *Mikado* to Baba the Turk's monologue? . . . I fear there will always remain an imbalance between the highly ramified and allusive intelligence of Auden and the bare and almost abstract intelligence of the later Stravinsky. . . . September 10. From a box in La Fenice I watched the dress rehearsal of the *Rake*. [Ferdinand] Leitner conducted like a man of experience; tomorrow when the composer takes the podium, they say it will all be more muted. I do not pretend to do a critique of the new music of Stravinsky, but I cannot help but greet with pleasure the reappearance after so many years of an opera that has *parts* for the singers. . . . Another pleasant novelty is the elimination of the big orchestra, the symphonic padding. Here the Devil comes on to the accompaniment of a harpsichord, and it is enough. . . . September 11. Great triumph for *The Rake's Progress* at La Fenice. Stravinsky is led out to the footlights where he bobs like a rubber puppet. When he directs, busy and absent, with large, imprecise

66 *September 5, 1951*. Arriving in Venice. L. to r.: Vera Arturovna, Auden, I.S., Lipnitzky (the Paris photographer), Kallman, Ferdinando Ballo (Director of the Biennale di Venezia).

67

67 *September 5, 1951*. Venice. The man behind Stravinsky is Emanuel Menkes, who sang the part of the Keeper in Bedlam in the opera.

According to my diary, after installing ourselves in the Bauer Grünwald, we went to Florian's, where Auden talked eloquently about Venice in *The Wings of the Dove*. On September 6, Act II was rehearsed in the Teatro La Fenice in the afternoon, Act III in the evening. The Stravinskys' luncheon guests in the next days included Nadia Boulanger, Marcelle Meyer, Nicolas Nabokov, Igor Markevitch. The Stravinskys returned to Milan on September 23.

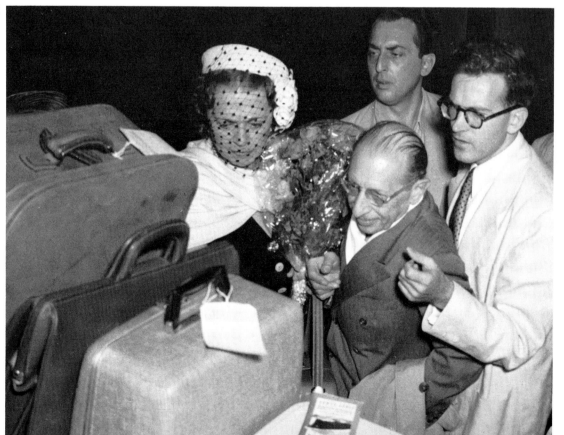

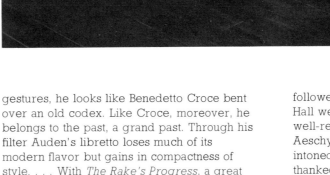

gestures, he looks like Benedetto Croce bent over an old codex. Like Croce, moreover, he belongs to the past, a grand past. Through his filter Auden's libretto loses much of its modern flavor but gains in compactness of style. . . . With *The Rake's Progress*, a great European by adoption admonishes Europeans not to make barbarians of themselves. I predict, however, that many Europeans will continue to write boring music dramas, not operas architecturally constructed like a chamber sonata. September 12. Reception put on by the City in Stravinsky's honor. He proceeds to the Embarcadero, in the Rialto,

followed by his entourage. In a room in City Hall we crowd around the Mayor, who gives a well-received speech in which the names of Aeschylus, Hugo, and Arrigo Boito are intoned. Stravinsky, seated, received and thanked. He bows like a Russian in a sort of swan dive. I had the opportunity to exchange a few words with him and was not surprised to find him so simple and humanly solitary. Fame, Hollywood, and dollars have left untouched his essential nature of a little *barin* who is afraid of the Devil and would like all of life to be a beautiful opera closer to Tchaikovsky than to Wagner.''

After the premiere of *The Rake's Progress*, Stravinsky spent two months concertizing in Europe. On his return to Milan, September 23, he wrote to Hans Rosbaud in Baden-Baden: "The sojourn in Venice was a hell for me. I was literally swamped." Stravinsky was even busier after Venice. In Milan, he conducted concerts on September 29 and October 1 (Symphony in Three Movements, *Petrushka* Suite, *Norwegian Moods*, *Circus Polka*, *Divertimento*). On October 2, the Stravinskys took the train to Basel and slept there (Hotel Three Kings). They spent the next day in the museum and left for Cologne on a train that arrived at 11 p.m. The first and last pieces (*Symphonies of Winds*, *Oedipus Rex*) in Stravinsky's program there, October 8, were recorded on the 9th by Columbia Records. The other work, *Apollo*, had to be cut to 22 minutes to fit a broadcast, and it may be worth mentioning that Stravinsky chose to omit the music from No. 39 to No. 63. The following week, in Baden-Baden, was enlivened by a visit from Nicolas Nabokov and by an excursion in the Schwarzwald with Count Salm, the Grünewald scholar. Stravinsky caught a cold, however, and, convincing him that he needed a rest, his wife canceled his concert in Lausanne, which would have taken place between those in Munich and Geneva. Tension mounted before his Geneva appearance, for the reason that Ernest Ansermet was scheduled to conduct *Orpheus*

twice in the week before Stravinsky's concert featuring the same piece. Stravinsky knew this weeks before, and had written from Milan to Roger Vuataz, Director of Radio-Geneva, not mentioning Ansermet's name: "I want to perform *Orpheus* in Geneva myself and I do not care what others do." When Stravinsky and Ansermet encountered each other accidentally in a streetcar during the composer's first day in Geneva, the two former friends drank tea together and set a date for dinner. Stravinsky did not attend Ansermet's concert, but sent me in his place. (I sat with Mme Ansermet during a too-slow performance of *Orpheus* and a well-paced one of Beethoven's Violin Concerto—with Isaac Stern, whom Stravinsky met for the first time in the lobby of the Hôtel des Bergues.) On November 4, in Victoria Hall, which, according to the *Journal de Genève*, was not full, Stravinsky conducted *Orpheus*, *Norwegian Moods*, *Circus Polka*, and the *Divertimento*. He attended a reception afterward at which Ansermet was present, though the conversation I remember most clearly was between the composer and Denis de Rougemont. On November 5, the Stravinskys left by train for Rome. In Milan, at midnight, while changing to a sleeping-car, the composer was met by a delegation from La Scala (headed by Antonio Giringhelli) asking him to choose the prize-winning opera from among one hundred and thirty(!) scores

submitted. Having agreed weeks before to join Honegger and Pizzetti as a judge in the contest, Stravinsky ran his finger along a list of the composers and nominated his friend, Juan Jose Castro. The Rome program on the 7th, in the Teatro Argentina, consisted of the Symphony in Three Movements, String Concerto, *Apollo*, *Scherzo à la Russe*—described in a review as music "*finlandese*"—*Moods*, *Circus Polka*, *Divertimento*. On the 11th, the Stravinskys went to Naples for a concert (15th), for which he received his fee only a year later and after an extensive correspondence. Back in Rome (16th), he conducted a benefit concert (in the Teatro Argentina: *Petrushka* Suite, *Divertimento*, *Firebird* Suite) for flood victims, an obligation to the Accademia di Santa Cecilia, of which he was a member and which in 1950 awarded him the lucrative Busoni Prize. The Stravinskys spent November 20 exploring Hadrian's Villa and the next day flew to New York, with stops in Paris, Shannon, and Boston. Auden and Isherwood met the Stravinsky plane at Idlewild and dined with them—it was Thanksgiving—at the Lombardy Hotel. On November 25, after two rehearsals, Stravinsky conducted the New York City Ballet in *Le Baiser de la fée*. On the 26th and 28th, he attended ballet performances, liking *Tyl Eulenspiegel*, detesting *The Miraculous Mandarin*. On the 29th, the Stravinskys saw *Apollo* and *Firebird*.

70 *September 5, 1951*. The Grand Canal, Venice.

71 *October 10, 1951, 4:30 p.m.* Baden-Oos. Herr and Frau Heinrich Strobel meet the Stravinskys arriving on the Rheingold-Express from Cologne. In Baden-Baden, on October 14, Stravinsky conducted his Ode, Symphony in C, *Scènes de Ballet*, and *Petrushka* Suite. On the 15th, Mrs. Stravinsky wrote to her stepdaughter in California: ''Yesterday's concert was a huge success. We will stay here and rest for two more days. The place is charming, a true *station balnéaire*. Naturally papa has had to go to the doctor every day, having lost his voice as a result of the cold that he caught in Cologne. He is so careful to avoid drafts, he eats prudently, he has vitamin injections, yet he is always catching something. Now he has a cough and is afraid of bronchitis.'' On October 17, the Stravinskys drove to Stuttgart and completed the journey from there to Munich by train.

71

72

72 *October 20, 1956*. Deutsches Museum, Munich. Stravinsky had six rehearsals for his Munich concert of October 21 (*Orpheus*, *Oedipus Rex*). In June 1956, the critic Walter Panofsky (*Süddeutsche Zeitung*) had written to him asking for a comment on the statement that the ideal conductor would resemble a bell-ringer. Stravinsky answered (June 7) that, although the remark was not his but C.F. Ramuz's, ''there is some truth in it. Nevertheless, *I* am not at all trying to bind the musical performer on the simpleness of a bell-ringer.''

On October 22, the Stravinskys went by train to St. Gall. During part of the trip, two ladies sharing the compartment with them discussed Stravinsky's concert of the previous evening, then, suddenly recognizing him, offered embarrassed apologies.

Shortly after the Venice premiere of *The Rake's Progress*, Rudolf Bing asked Stravinsky for permission to present the opera at the Metropolitan Opera. The composer accepted in principle and discussions took place immediately after his return to New York. At Bing's invitation, the Stravinskys attended performances at the Metropolitan of *Die Fledermaus* (November 10); *Figaro* (December 3; Stravinsky admired Fritz Reiner's conducting and Cesare Siepi's singing); *Rigoletto* (December 8; Stravinsky purchased one of Eugene Berman's costume designs at an exhibition a few days later); and *Cosi fan tutte* (December 28; on the strength of Blanche Thebom's performance in this opera, Stravinsky invited her to sing the part of Baba the Turk in his own). Stravinsky wrote to Bing from Hollywood (January 14, 1952), proposing Elisabeth Schwarzkopf for the part of Anne Trulove. Bing answered (January 16): "For reasons I would rather not discuss in writing, the lady you mentioned cannot be considered for the Metropolitan Opera." On January 27, Chester Kallman sent Stravinsky a letter setting forth the arguments against concluding Act II with the Auction Scene. Stravinsky answered (January 31) that, when he had been in New York, "all minds seemed quite set on the solution of four scenes"; but he left the decision to the librettists. Sending a copy of Kallman's letter to Balanchine (February 2), Stravinsky reminded him that Auden had agreed to the four-scenes-in-Act II solution and must have been converted by Kallman on his return to New York. (Stravinsky wanted to avoid a pause between the Auction and Graveyard scenes in Act III.) Balanchine favored the apportioning of scenes as written (letter of February 6).

The first performance of the *Rake*, at the Met, Saturday afternoon, February 14, 1953, was preceded by a dress rehearsal (February 12) for an audience of 1,200. *The New York Times* reported: "A lectern with an electric light attached to it was set up for Stravinsky in one of the center aisles near the pit, and during the first two acts he stood and followed the score. . . . Several times he dashed over to whisper suggestions to Mr. Reiner." The program booklet for the premiere contained a note by Auden and Kallman to the effect that they had always had two things in mind, an idea of a certain kind of music which would suggest a rhythmical or prosodic pattern, and such poets of the period as Pope,

Gay, Swift, and Smart. The note also credits Geoffrey Gorer with the suggestion that a spade be the second card in the Graveyard Scene.

At the premiere, the Stravinskys were seated in a loge. (I sat with Alma Mahler and Dr. Paco Lagerstrom, a few rows from the orchestra.) The performance was heard by a large radio audience that included Aldous Huxley, who wrote to Stravinsky: "*Cher ami*, in spite of the 3,000 miles of separation, we had great pleasure, at least by broadcast, in attending the premiere of the *Rake*. The broadcast was good enough except that the choruses were a little feeble and anaemic, a matter, I suppose, of microphone placement. Nevertheless, everything was beautiful. The memory of the opera, heard in the morning, fortified us in the afternoon, when we went to show Edith Sitwell the horrors—more obscene than ever—of Forest Lawn. Love from all of us. *Amicalement* and with all my admiration, Aldous Huxley." (Original in French.)

Another letter, from Maryla Friedlander, Hotel Marseilles, New York, reminded Stravinsky that "the name 'Baba' means 'father' in Turkish and cannot be used in connection with a woman. . . . Perhaps the name is a wonderful coincidence. Many years ago a relative of my mother in Ustilug told me that not far from your relatives' home was a property which, no doubt, you have visited. I remember that my mother's relatives, who came from Kovel, called her 'Baba.' I did not understand this, since I had heard that the name Baba might have been fashionable then in that part of Russia and that such things often impress themselves into creative processes." The mother of Stravinsky's sister-in-law, born in Kiev, was called "Baba Anya."

73, 74 On October 27, 1952, Sarah Caldwell of Boston University's Opera Workshop wrote to Stravinsky inviting him to conduct *The Rake's Progress* there after the performances of the Metropolitan Opera. He answered (November 10), naming a large fee and requesting that this be kept confidential, "since in any place but a university I would be obliged to ask double the amount." Miss Caldwell discussed the project with him in the Gladstone Hotel (New York) on January 9, 1953. An agreement was reached whereby he would conduct a public dress rehearsal on May 17 and a performance on May 18. On February 3, he auditioned Miss Caldwell's singers.

(Stravinsky was in Baltimore, February 15–19, for a concert, and he led the New York Philharmonic in concerts on the 26th and 27th.) Early in March, realizing that a second performance would be "popularly demanded," Boston University offered Stravinsky a large bonus to conduct it. He accepted, and flew to California on March 11 (after the final recording session of the *Rake* with the Metropolitan Opera). On March 29, he left again, to conduct concerts in Havana and Caracas, and on April 28, flew from Venezuela to New York, continuing, on May 2, to Boston (Sheraton Plaza Hotel). On May 4, he auditioned the cast and, according to the *Boston Herald* (May 5), was pleased. The newspaper also quoted Miss Caldwell: "Baba, the Bearded Lady . . . as Stravinsky presents her, is not merely a ludicrous figure, but also a cruelly afflicted woman with a certain pathetic dignity of her own." After the first Boston performance, Stravinsky telegraphed Edward James (who had accompanied him to Baltimore for the February 18 concert): "Both your good wishes and your beautiful present which I wear when I am conducting *Rake* brought me good luck and a real ovation. . . . Love Str." The second performance (May 19), with a different cast, was a disaster, however, and Stravinsky, ill for two weeks with colitis, was obliged to cancel a concert in Chicago. On his recovery, the Stravinskys drove to California, arriving at their home on June 4.

To celebrate Stravinsky's seventy-fifth birthday, Miss Caldwell helped to organize three concerts of his music presented on Boston Commons, June 28, 29 and 30, 1957. The program consisted of the Greeting Prelude, Symphony in Three Movements, Capriccio (with Soulima Stravinsky as soloist), *Renard* (in the New York City Ballet staging), and the *Petrushka* Suite. On May 18, the composer wrote to his sons: "I have finally finished my ballet *Agon*, and Bob will conduct the premiere on June 17. I will probably record it the next day. I am not sure Vera and I will attend my concerts in Boston conducted by Bob with Soulima at the piano (Capriccio). We want very much to go, and, furthermore, our round-trip tickets would be paid for, but we do not want to fly anymore. . . . At the end of July we will be in Sante Fe, where Bob conducts the *Rake*. From there to New York, where we catch the *Ile de France* to Plymouth. We are invited to Dartington where Bob is conducting my music."

73 *May 16, 1953.* Boston. Reception by the President of Boston University for the composer of *The Rake's Progress*.

74 *May 1953.* Boston. With Sarah Caldwell.

KANONISCHES ADAGIO
für 2 Bassethörner und Fagott
von
W. A. MOZART
Köch. Verz. Nº 410

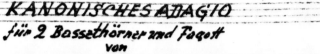

75, 76 Mozart's canonic *Adagio* (Vienna, 1783) for Two Basset Horns and Bassoon, copied by Stravinsky in January 1952.

77 *May 1952*. Paris. Théâtre des Champs-Elysées. Stravinsky applauds Pierre Monteux's performance of *Le Sacre du printemps*. Arthur Sachs is seated at the composer's right.

78, 79, 80 *March 1952*. Hollywood. Photographs taken in the home of Stravinsky's daughter, Milene Marion.

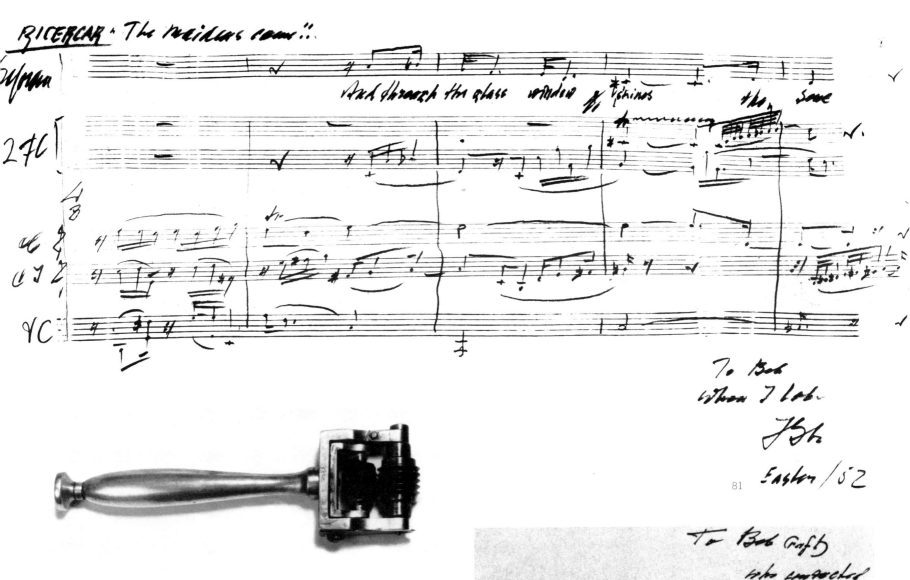

81 *Easter 1952.* Sketch for the re-instrumentation of *The Maidens Came* to include oboe and English horn.

82 Stravinsky's styluses. The larger one was kept on the music rack of his piano. He carried the smaller one (shown with its cover) in his pocket, and used it when away from home. He designed both instruments in his early Swiss years.

igor strawinsky
three songs
from
william shakespeare

85

85, 86 On July 5, 1953, I gave Stravinsky a copy of Shakespeare's Sonnet, "Musick to Heare," suggesting that he set it for soprano with accompaniment of flute, harp, and guitar (Mrs. Stravinsky had bought a guitar and was learning to play it from manuals provided by Sol Babitz). On July 16, Stravinsky showed me the completed song, scored, however, for flute, clarinet, and viola. (I did not tell him until November 16 that he had omitted a word from the sonnet, as well as two lines from the song, "When Daisies Pied"—oversights that he quickly repaired, in the case of the song with the addition of a single measure.) On July 21, Stravinsky attended a read-through rehearsal of his Septet at the home of Peter (Evenings on the Roof) Yates. After twelve days in the hospital (July 23–August 3) for a prostatectomy, Stravinsky resumed work on his "Three Songs from William Shakespeare." (**86**) Sketch-score of "Full Fadom Five."

86

igor strawinsky

88 *December 1953.* Fanfare, originally the beginning of *Agon.*

89 *June 1, 1954.* Stravinsky had gone to Lisbon for a concert, while I returned from Europe to California to conduct the Ojai Festival. Note his descriptions of color, and that he was reading Dylan Thomas's play, perhaps with a view to composing music for it.

90 Manuscript cover for the instrumentation of the 1911 piano accompaniment of the Balmont songs.

91 *October 19, 1953.* Record label of three of the pieces performed at a concert of Stravinsky's jazz: *Ragtime for eleven instruments,* Three Dances from *Histoire du soldat,* and the Piano-Rag Music (played by Ingolf Dahl).

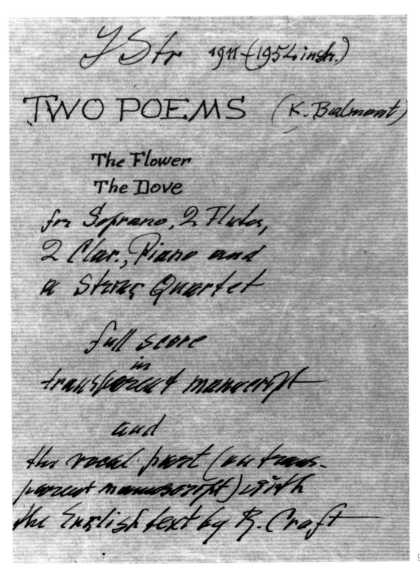

89

90

91

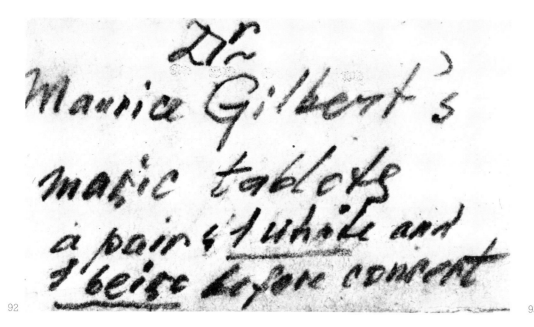

92

Good luck to Bob
POCKET SCORES
IS
Feb/54

IGOR STRAWINSKY
SEPTET

93

92 *February 21, 1954.* Hollywood. The white pill was a tranquilizer, the beige a stimulant. The combination was prepared by a Geneva doctor to allay Stravinsky's anxieties during concerts. He gave me a packet of the pills on February 21, 1954, just before I conducted George Antheil's *Ballet mécanique.*

On April 2–3, 1954, the Stravinskys flew from New York to Rome. On Sunday, April 4, they spent the afternoon at Frascati, Albano, Rocca di Papa, returning to Rome for a party at the American Academy with Poulenc, Samuel Barber, Henze, the Elliott Carters, and others. On April 5, the Stravinskys visited Caprarola, Villa Lante, and Bomarzo. In the evening, in Rome's Foro Italico, they heard Darius Milhaud conduct Satie's *Socrate.* On April 6, they explored Cerveteri and Tarquinia. They spent most of the 7th in the Villa Giulia, going at night to see Henze's *Boulevard Solitude* at the Rome Opera. Stravinsky and I were refused admittance, however, because we were not wearing black ties. An exception was made when the attendant recognized the composer, but he chose to return to the hotel with me. During the fracas in the lobby, Nicolas Nabokov punched a guard, thereby provoking a free-for-all. Later that night, the Mayor of Rome sent flowers to Mrs. Stravinsky, but by this time the story was on the front page of *The New York Times.* On April 8, the Stravinskys drove to Tivoli. Afterward, in the Hassler Hotel, they visited with the Roland-Manuels. On the 9th, they returned to the Villa Giulia and dined with the Nabokovs. Rehearsals, concerts, and *La Cenerentola* at the Opera occupied the 10th and 11th. On the 12th, I conducted Stravinsky's Septet in the Teatro Eliseo. On the 14th, Stravinsky conducted *Orpheus, Scherzo à la Russe,* and *Firebird* in the Foro Italico. (On the 15th and 16th, I conducted the Scarlatti Orchestra in Naples in pieces by Mozart, Bach, Schubert, and Webern.) In Rome, on April 17, the Stravinskys dined with

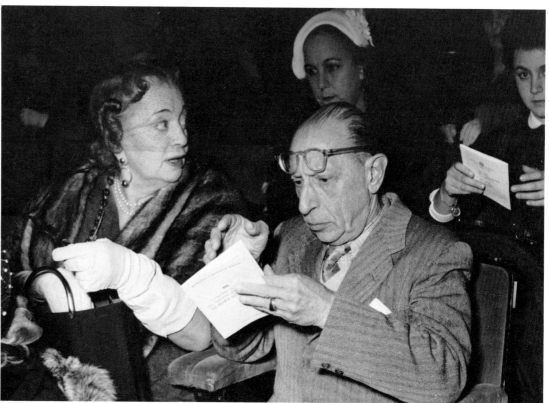

94

the Caetanis in their palace on the Botteghe Oscure. On the 19th, Stravinsky and his son-in-law left by train for Turin, while Stravinsky's daughter and I visited Subiaco, Carsolì, and Rieti. On the 20th, Mrs. Stravinsky and I went to Ninfa, Norma, and the Caetani Palace at Sermoneta. From the 21st to the 28th, Mrs. Stravinsky, her stepdaughter, and I were in Siena, Pisa, Lucca, and Florence. We joined Stravinsky in Lugano on the evening of the 28th.

Rome spring 1954
while Bob
[illegible] my
Septet

95

96

CLASS OF SERVICE

This is a full-rate Telegram or Cable-gram unless its deferred character is indicated by a suitable symbol above or preceding the address.

WESTERN UNION

W. P. MARSHALL, PRESIDENT

FX-1201

SYMBOLS

DL=Day Letter

NL=Night Letter

LT=Int'l Letter Telegram

VLT=Int'l Victory Ltr.

The filing time shown in the date line on telegrams and day letters is STANDARD TIME at point of origin. Time of receipt is STANDARD TIME at point of destination

1954 SEP 20 PM 3 13

LA172 OC523 LA555 L.WLA191

(O.BHB401) PD=BEVERLY HILLS CAIF 20 1115AMP=

ROBERT CRAFT MONDAY EVENIN GCONCERTS (

WEST HOLLYWOOD AUD 647 NORTH SAN VICENTE BLVD

LOSA=

WISHING YOU TO HAVE AS MUCH PERSONAL ENJOYMENT AS YOU

WILL BE GIVING US TONIGHT SHOULD PROVE TO BE YOUR FINEST

REWARD FOR JOB SO REMARKABLY DONE. AFFECTIONATE THOUGHTS

=IGOR STRAVINSKY=(

THE COMPANY WILL APPRECIATE SUGGESTIONS FROM ITS PATRONS CONCERNING ITS SERVICE

97

94, 96 *April 12, 1954.* Teatro Eliseo, Rome. Before and after the performance of the Septet.

On March 15, 1954, Lawrence Morton wrote to Stravinsky: ''Bob and I have talked about the performances of your new piece on the Dylan Thomas text. . . .'' Stravinsky gave his consent to the plans, and on August 8, *The Los Angeles Times* published an interview with Stravinsky by Albert Goldberg: ''*Instead of an Opera with Dylan Thomas, Stravinsky Writes Memorial to Poet.* . . . Dylan Thomas's visit was eagerly anticipated in the Stravinsky household. On the very day of his expected arrival, last November 9, the doorbell rang: 'We had expected to see Mr. Thomas,' Mrs. Stravinsky recalled, 'but there stood a Western Union messenger. We were a little startled, for we cannot forget the old days in Russia when a telegram only meant disaster. Then we laughed, thinking it was probably just another invitation to a party. . . .' 'We had nothing definite planned,' says Stravinsky. 'It would have been simple, no conceits and no poetic indulgence. We had talked of an allegory—perhaps the discovery of language. Or a man and a tree, or their relationship. It was all very vague. Thomas was so gifted and so versatile that he could have evolved a new form. He was a man who understood so well the theater and the nature of the theater. For the moment I have no appetite for another opera.''' *In Memoriam Dylan Thomas* was performed twice in a Monday Evening Concert, September 20, 1954, in the Los Angeles County Auditorium (West Hollywood). The program began with a Ricercare by Andrea Gabrieli, Purcell's Funeral Music for Queen Mary, a Ricercare by Willaert, Schütz's *Fili mi Absalon*, and six Gesualdo madrigals. Aldous Huxley read a paper, ''A word about Dylan Thomas.'' (*The Los Angeles Examiner* reported, September 22, that ''Huxley directed attention [to] Thomas's genius in establishing 'the ineffable, mysterious relationships between fact and symbol' and he concluded with the remark, 'God help a generation which does not read its poets.''') A recording followed of Thomas reading three of his poems, and the program concluded with Bach's Cantata No. 106, *Gottes Zeit ist die allerbeste Zeit.* According to *The Los Angeles Herald and Express*, September 21, ''Robert Craft . . . warned the audience quaintly that 'what seem to be wrong notes are Gesualdo's right ones.''' One of the madrigal singers was Marilyn Horne.

98

98 *April 30, 1954*. Stresa. Stravinsky conducted a concert in Lugano on the 29th, and on the morning of the 30th went by car to Lago Maggiore, crossed by ferry to Intra, and lunched in the Milano Hotel. His train from Stresa to Geneva left at 4 p.m., by which time it was lightly raining.

100 *October 20, 1954*. Hollywood.

PULCINELLA

BALLET

Bob Craft 1954

99

101 *1954.* Hollywood. Photograph by Michael Barrie.

102 *March 10, 1955.* Pittsburgh. The photograph was taken during a rehearsal of the Pittsburgh Symphony. The Stravinskys had left Los Angeles, March 5, by train, arriving in Pittsburgh at midnight, March 8. Stravinsky conducted two concerts there, on March 11 and 13 (matinée), with a program of his *Scènes de Ballet* and *Petrushka* Suite, Serenades by Mozart (K. 239) and Tchaikovsky. After the second concert, the Stravinskys flew to New York in the late evening, and the next day to Lisbon.

101

103, 104 "After a boring opera in the Shrein [Shrine] Auditorium Nov/55 with Edw[ard] James."

105 *April 15, 1955.* Galleria Obelisco, Rome. On March 27, 1955, the Stravinskys flew from Madrid to Rome, where the composer conducted a concert on April 6. The purpose of the trip was the exhibition of Mrs. Stravinsky's paintings, but an attack of diverticulitis prevented Stravinsky from attending the vernissage. He was hospitalized (Sanatrix, via di Trasconi) from April 12 to 14, after treatment from Drs. Pietro Valdoni and Prof. Ugo Peratoner.

108, 109 *June 1956.* Leaving New York on the S.S. *Vulcania.*

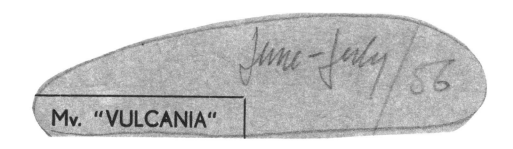

Mv. "VULCANIA"   June-July/56

7 49th Vora   Cab. Nr. 118

108

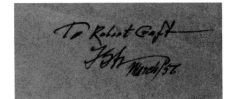

106

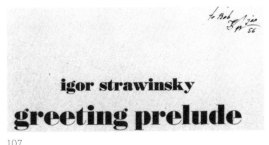

igor strawinsky
greeting prelude

107

109

51

111

110 *July 1956.* Athens, lobby of the Grande Bretagne Hotel.

111 *July 15, 1956.* Athens. Climbing the Acropolis with Lawrence Morton.

112 *August 1956.* Venice. With Lawrence Morton, the façade of Saint Moses in the background.

113, 114 *July 5, 1956.* Gibraltar. Photographs by Lawrence Morton.

112

113

114

116

115 First page of the full score of Stravinsky's instrumentation of Bach's *Vom Himmel hoch*. The chorale was added later.

116, 117 *September 1956*. Venice. The Stravinskys and Alessandro Piovesan attend a concert.

117

118

118 *September 13, 1956.* Venice. In St. Mark's Basilica before the premiere of the *Canticum Sacrum*, with Theodore Stravinsky and Count Massimo d'Alessio.

119 *Venice.* Entering the Taverna Fenice after the premiere of the *Canticum Sacrum*.

120 *September 13, 1956.* St. Mark's Basilica. Eugenio Montale wrote, "Venice, September 14, 1956: I saw Stravinsky come out of his hotel and head for the Frezzerie; no one tried to stop and pester him, but many turned around to follow him with their eyes. Having pestered the maestro on other occasions, . . . this time I did not renew the attack.

"Stravinsky has theorized plenty, but he is not a theoretician; he is more of an experimenter. So it is not surprising that after expressing his disapproval of serial music, he would have turned to twelve-tone technique for a substantial portion of the three hundred measures of his *Canticum*, not neglecting 'the crab' (the repetition of the row in reverse order) or 'the mirror,' a perspective and spatial refraction of the row. . . . But crab and mirror are at home in Venice. People here will be curious what inspiration the grand old man was able to find in the figure of Saint Mark, which he sums up in verses taken from the Gospel According to Saint Mark and the Old Testament. The truth is that Saint Mark has nothing to do with it. The work is a eulogy of Venice that the Orthodox Stravinsky, not unmindful of the Byzantine character of his other religious music, intended to compose. And with regard to technique, he has recently affirmed that for him all techniques are good.

The use of the serial row may have clothed Stravinsky's music in a more modern dress, but the substance of the *Canticum* for Saint Mark performed yesterday evening in the Basilica remains unchanged. . . . The text, excerpted from here and there in the Old and New Testaments, and supposed to form a poem indicating 'the Structures of the Church Evangelical,' centers around the 'Trinity of Virtues.' . . . We listen and we see skillfully functioning structures. . . . The *Canticum* begins with a modal dedication, a duet between tenor and baritone with trombone accompaniment; there follows a verse that 'represents the tie with Stravinsky's past,' and then the twelve-tone row is stated with 'Surge, Aquilo,' sung by a tenor: a melismatic passage that recalls Elizabethan music. . . . At intervals the three virtues—Charity, Hope, Faith—are introduced, with dialogue among the soloists and chorus and choral canons in the soprano and bass parts. Here the twelve-tone row roves at will. Then follows a fourth movement in three parts. It passes from the *cantus firmus*, sung by the baritone, to an interlude that is the retrograde form of the row, to a four-part canon and a new inversion of the row performed by the baritone (assisted by two trombones). The retrograde inversion brings us to the final coda without dangerous bumps or jerks. The short journey lasts seventeen minutes. . . . Dynamism, the capacity to move sounds, has always been Stravinsky's fundamental quality. The choruses in *Canticum* give one more demonstration of that. . . . The program did not end there. Stravinsky had us listen to his

119

transcription of the Bach *Canonic Variations* on the Christmas chorale, *Vom Himmel hoch.* It is an instrumental arrangement that is actually a bold reworking. To round out the program, the following pieces were performed, conducted by Robert Craft: two *Ricercari* by Andrea Gabrieli, for four trombones; *In Ecclesiis benedicite Domine* by Giovanni Gabrieli; *Lauda Jerusalem* and *Pulchra es amica mea* by Monteverdi; and *Deutsches Konzert* by Heinrich Schütz. In addition to the soloists already named, we should also mention Marilyn Horne, Magda Laszlo. . . ."

19 Spt/57 Venezia

Red crpsc. 4.500.000
Hmter 55

20 Spt/57 Bleedms
(13 unges)
Blood tension 168/95

23 Spt/57
Red crpsc. 4.500.000
Hmter 52

Dr Protetch New York

7 Nov/57

Red crpsc. 5.700.000
Hmter. 54

8 Nov/57
Bleedms
16 onzes

11 Nov/57
Red crpsc 4.900.000

Hmter 52

Dr Knauer Hollywood
after 9 visits

5 Dec/57

Red crpsc. 4.900.000

Hmter. 44

Jan 17/58 Red crpsc.
5.300.000
Hmter 50

Feb 28/58 Red crpsc
5.600.000
Hmter 55

March

March 10/58
Red crpsc.
5.600.000
Hmter. 53

April 4/58
Red crpsc.
6.100.000
Hmter 56

121 *1957–1958*. One of Stravinsky's records of his blood tests.

122 *October 14, 1956*. In the Red Cross Hospital, Munich. On November 3, Mrs. Stravinsky wrote to me in Paris: "Jackie [Marilyn Horne, who had been with the Stravinskys helping out as a secretary] wrote to me that she is expecting you in Vienna very soon. . . . My husband wants to order tickets for Rome and I asked the agency here. The best train is at 11:30 p.m., arriving the next day at 2 p.m. Very difficult to have tickets in the sleeping car. How I would like to be home and not to go through this ordeal of traveling with a sick man. I never in my life was so lonesome and so sad. Merde for your concert. It will be a big success, I am sure. Much love, V."

123 *June 1957*. 1260 North Wetherly Drive. Pause during a televised interview in NBC's Wisdom series.

124 *May 1957*. Hollywood.

125 *June 1957*. Hollywood. Recording *Agon*.

123

124

125

ALDOUS HUXLEY *and* THE GESUALDO MADRIGALISTS

Robert Craft, conductor

Grace-Lynn Martin, Marilyn Horne, sopranos
Cora Lauridsen, contralto
Richard Robinson, tenor
Charles Scharbach, bass

I.   Four Madrigals by Carlo Gesualdo, Prince of Venosa
     Dolcissima mia vita   (c. 1560-1613)
     O dolorosa gioia
     Meraviglia d'amore
     Moro lasso

II. Mr. Huxley, speaking on "The Court of Ferrara and
     Gesualdo."

III. Four Madrigals by Gesualdo
     Ardo per te
     Tu piangi
     Ardita zanzaretta
     Luci serene e chiare

INTERMISSION

IV. A. Two Arias by Claudio Monteverdi (1567-1643)
       Lasciatemi morire
       Partenza amoroso

Miss Horne

    B. Solo Ballata by Heinrich Isaac (c. 1450-1517)
       Mostrarsi ardirata di fore

Mr. Robinson

    C. Four Madrigals by Gesualdo
       Ecco moriro dunque
       Tu m'uccidi o crudele
       Io tacero
       Itene o miei sospiri

This program is produced by the Monday Evening Concerts
of Los Angeles

127

Santa Barbara News-Press, Sunday Morning, March 4, 1956

Two men of genius, composer Igor Stravinsky (left) and writer Aldous Huxley, are shown as they inspect the Schott Doll Collection during their recent tour of the Art Museum.—News-Press photo

126

128

128 The Gesualdo Madrigalists at 1260 North Wetherly Drive.

129 *May 1955*. Radio Recorders (Los Angeles). The sopranos are Grace-Lynn Martin and Marilyn Horne. Stravinsky, Edward James, and Ruth Adams (Gesualdo scholar) are in the control room.

129

Illumina nos
from the book (1603) of
SACRAE CANTIONES
for 6 and 7 voices,

from the book (1603) of SACRAE CANTIONES
for six and seven voices, the missing Six-
tus and Bassus parts composed by

IGOR STRAVINSKY

130–133 On May 5, 1957, Stravinsky completed his composition of the lost Sextus and Bassus parts of Gesualdo's only seven-voice motet. A week or so before, I had transcribed the five completed part books (1603) and asked Stravinsky to add the missing voices. He enjoyed doing this and naturally could not resist writing over my manuscript. The reader will easily distinguish Stravinsky's calligraphy from my scrawl, unimproved examples of which can be seen in the Tenor, measures 7 and 8 (the C and G); in the Septima pars, measures 14 through 17; and in the Quintus, measures 12–13, and 17. Beginning at measure 18, Stravinsky began to compose the two added parts in a three-staff score.

131

Enlighten us, God of Mercies, by the Seven-
fold Grace of the Paraclete so that, through
it, liberated from the darkness of sin, we may
partake of the glory of life.

(Translation supplied by Ernst Krenek)

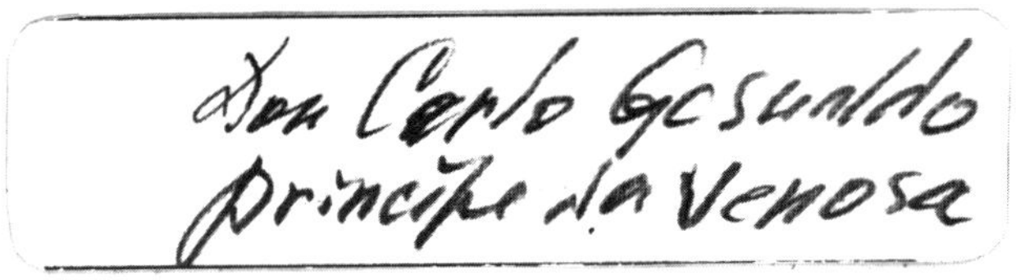

Don Carlo Gesualdo
principe da Venosa

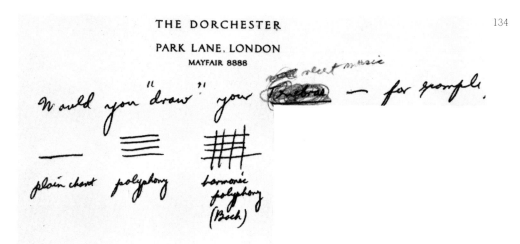

THE DORCHESTER

PARK LANE, LONDON
MAYFAIR 8888

134

135

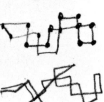

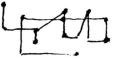

136

134, 135 *August 23, 1957.* The photograph of the original of Stravinsky's response to my request to "draw" his music contains the five rejected versions as well as the final one. The photograph also shows that, about this date, he had considered the title "Tenebrae" for *Threni.* (**135**) Stravinsky's re-drawing of his pictorializations of musical styles.

136 *August 19, 1957.* Bath. With H.D.F. Kitto.

On August 1, 1957, the Stravinskys sailed from New York on the S.S. *Liberté,* bound for Plymouth and a fortnight in Dartington. They debarked on the morning of the 7th and in the afternoon rented a car in Torquay. The next day they drove to Exeter, and the day after took the train to London (Dorchester Hotel), where they spent most of the 10th in the

Victoria and Albert Museum. On the 11th, I rehearsed for a BBC broadcast concert, after which we visited the British Museum. On the 12th, following a recording session in Maida Vale, we returned to Dartington, by train to Newton Abbot and from there by car. On the 14th, I conducted a concert in the Banquet Hall, Dartington. On the 16th, Stravinsky

visited Roberto Gerhard, who played a tape of his Symphony. The same evening, I conducted Bach's *Aus der Tiefe* in a Totnes church; the Stravinskys, in the audience, sat with Julian Huxley (an old friend) and Arthur Waley. On the 17th, the Stravinskys and I drove to Tintagel. On the 18th, I conducted a second Stravinsky concert in the Banquet Hall. The next day, we lunched in Bath (St. Francis Hotel) with H.D.F. Kitto, returning to Dartington by way of Wells and Glastonbury. On the 20th, I conducted two performances of *Histoire du soldat,* Christopher Hassall narrating.

While at Dartington, Stravinsky was photographed by Gjon Mili for *Life* magazine. On the 21st, Mili accompanied him to Stonehenge, Salisbury, and London, joining him again next month in Venice. On August 22, the Stravinskys went to the Tate Gallery, and in the evening saw Agatha Christie's *The Mousetrap.* On August 24, they departed for Paris on the night train. Nabokov and Boulez were at the station, and some of the afternoon of the 25th was spent at the apartment of Boulez listening to him play Stockhausen's Piano Piece no. 11. That night the Stravinskys dined at La Pérouse with Nabokov, who discussed the participation of the Hamburg Radio Orchestra in Venice in the following year. The afternoon of the 26th was spent at Vega Records hearing test pressings, after which the Stravinskys left on the night train for Venice.

September 1957 was a happy month for the Stravinskys. Vera Arturovna painted, and Igor Fyodorovich composed the piece that on September 15 he was to call *Threni.* On September 2, the Stravinskys lunched with Giorgio de Chirico and his Russian-speaking wife, on September 4 visited Bill Congdon's studio near San Toma', and on the 8th were again with the Chiricos. On the 9th, the Stravinskys drove to Villa Malcontenta to see the Landsbergs. On the 11th, 12th, and 13th, the composer discussed programs with Nabokov and Rolf Liebermann. On the 14th, Marilyn Horne, en route to Rome, paid the Stravinskys a surprise visit. On the 15th, they went to Bologna with Mili. On the 18th, they explored the San Marco Museum. On the 19th, they dined with Congdon, and on the 20th attended a concert of music by Dallapiccola and Messiaen. At 1 a.m. on the 21st, Stravinsky received a call informing him of the death of Sibelius and asking for a comment ("Go to Hell"). On the 23rd, the Stravinskys went to Torcello with Congdon and Piovesan, stopping on the way at San Michele, where Vera Stravinsky placed flowers on Diaghilev's grave. (Stravinsky: "A pity Diaghilev could not appreciate it here.") On the 25th, the Stravinskys saw the Goldoni exhibition in the Palazzo Grassi, dining afterward with the Elliott Carters. The afternoon of the 26th was spent at Peggy Guggenheim's. On September 30, the Stravinskys drove to Munich via Heiligenblut and Zell-am-See.

137 *August 11, 1956.* With Eugene Berman at Villa Manin, Passariano.

138 *August 11, 1956.* At Villa Manin.

139, 140 *September 22, 1957.* At Villa Barbaro, Maser.

137

138

139

140

141, 142, 145 *September 1957.* Venice. Posing at a gondola station by the Hotel Bauer Grünwald.

143 *September 1957.* Venice. On the balcony of Stravinsky's room in the Hotel Bauer Grünwald.

144 *September 8, 1957.* Venice.

142

143

144

145

146

147

146, 148 *September 1957*. At the Palazzo
Podestà, Bologna.

147 *September 1957*. Venice. With Giorgio de
Chirico.

149 *June 1965*. The Vatican. Pope Paul VI, G.F.
Malipiero, and the Stravinskys, just before a
performance of *Symphony of Psalms*.

150 *September 22, 1957*. Asolo. At the home of
G.F. Malipiero.

151 *September 1958*. Venice, the Cavallino
Gallery. With G.F. Malipiero.

148

149

150

151

153

154 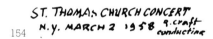 ST. THOMAS CHURCH CONCERT N.Y. MARCH 2 1958 R.Craft conducting

155

152 *October 1957.* Near Paris, with Pierre Suvchinsky.

155 *August 15, 1958.* Venice, San Servolo in the background.

156 *June 16, 1958.* Royce Hall, Los Angeles. Curtain call for the composer of *Mavra*, with Marni Nixon (Parasha) and Richard Robinson (Hussar).

156

Dear Bob, please insist this absurd bass-trumpet be replaced by my Flügelhorn called Bügel contralto in B(b); this is even more important (because of its solo in the beginning with the tenor) than the Sarrusophone problem. I make this request through you, because I am not quite sure to be understood by the Hund funk people what I am speaking about.

If possible please correct in *Canon a 3* at the end of bar 182 the 3 solos this way:

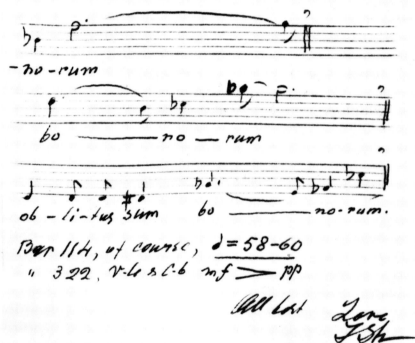

-no-rum

bo — no — rum

ob - li - tus sum bo — no-rum.

Bar 114, of course, ♩=58-60
" 322, v-ls & c-b mf > pp

All best Love ISt

157

158 *September 23, 1958*. Venice, Scuola di San Rocco. Stravinsky is about to conduct his *Symphonies of Wind Instruments*, followed by the first performance of *Threni*. The new work was surprisingly well received. *Time* Magazine (October 6) reported that the "big-name-studded audience (poet W.H. Auden, composer Francis Poulenc, et al.) braved a motorboat strike and journeyed by gondola to Venice's 450-year-old Scuola di San Rocco, one of Italy's famed Renaissance religious schools, for the fall's most eagerly awaited musical event. In hushed expectation, beneath a Tintoretto ceiling, they [*sic*] watched 76-year-old Igor Stravinsky, with a claw-like motion of his right hand, launch the orchestra into the premiere of his latest work. What followed was some of the finest—and most complex—music of Stravinsky's career. To prepare the Hamburg Radio Chorus for the taxing job of staying on pitch, while unaccompanied, conductor Robert Craft rehearsed the group more than twenty times." Another account is found in Eugenio Montale's diary for September 24, 1958: "Venice. One cannot help but be moved year after year by the sight of the elderly Stravinsky mounting the conductor's podium to present to the citizens of Venice (a city that now considers him an adopted son) and the habitués of the Festival the latest product of his study. The seventy-six-year-old maestro embodies fifty years of musical experience, and this imbues each of his reappearances with a warmth of feeling that overrides any purely critical considerations. No one, in fact, would have wanted to see him replaced yesterday evening by a conductor more expert than he is in the interpretation of Stravinskyan music even though in the dress rehearsal given yesterday afternoon for journalists, the frequent interruptions showed that the good preparatory work done by the young Craft in pulling it all together was thrown to the winds by the still younger Stravinsky, always unsure, always in search of himself. . . . Of the five elegies that go to make up the Lamentations of Jeremiah,

Stravinsky has set to music fragments of the first, third and fifth in the Latin. There are six soloists: soprano, alto, two tenors, a bass, and a basso profundo. The make-up of the orchestra is complex and rich in little-used instruments. The first fragment is broken up into five groups designated by Hebrew letters which are syllabized by the chorus; the chorus recites the whole text *sotto voce*, and it is then taken up by the tenor with counterpoint by the women's voices. And so it continues by groups, or sub-groups, for each of which the Hebrew letter is repeated. It would be too long and dry and also confusing to list all the devices that make up the structure of the work; this was explained here yesterday. . . . Maestro Roman Vlad, as competent as they come, following the 'fundamental twelve-tone constellation' of the work through all of its changes and bringing out the various songs to be found in it, the monody of the bass and all the architectonic symmetry to the final perfect consonance in which 'every motion of the soul is resolved.' Needless to say, here, as in the *Cantos* of Pound or the *Ulysses* of Joyce, the intelligence of the schema is of little assistance to one who listens, as the work should be listened to, with a kind of mental virginity. And the ingenuous impression left by *Threni* is this: that Stravinsky has not been suffocated by the technique and the format he has imposed on himself, for the score bears the stamp of his own personality, and he comes particularly alive whenever the undercurrent of normal tonality breaks as if by a miracle through the forest of discordant voices—which happens in many places with the chorus and in a few phrases with the soprano and alto. . . . We would not attempt to deny that from the complex of the sober and yet highly intricate score there emanates an afflatus of religious inspiration. Why should we deny to an intellect that has known all experience the right to a conversation with the Divine? . . .''

158

159, 160 *December 8, 1958*. London. Listening to a rehearsal of *Agon*, Robert Craft conducting the BBC Symphony. The rehearsals began December 3. The concert took place December 11.

1958 began pleasantly for the Stravinskys with a week in Houston, where Vera had an exhibition of her paintings, and where Igor conducted two concerts. After their return to Los Angeles, January 8, Stravinsky had a painful attack of bursitis and received upsetting reports about his blood disease. But, despite a bloodletting treatment on April 9, the next day he, his wife, and I drove to Carmel. On April 11, we visited San Juan Bautista and on the 12th continued to San Francisco (Clift Hotel), where he conducted concerts (*Apollo*, *Scherzo fantastique*, *Firebird*) on April 16, 17, and 18. On the afternoon of the 17th, the Stravinskys, William T. Brown, and I saw an exhibition of paintings by Afro at Mills College. After the matinée concert on the 18th, we returned to the Torres Inn, Carmel (and heard on the automobile radio that Ezra Pound had been released from St. Elizabeth's). On the 19th, we returned to Los Angeles.

Meanwhile, at the end of February, Alessandro Piovesan had died of pneumonia in Venice. His successor, Giovanni Ponti, soon began to revise the plans for the Hamburg-sponsored *Threni* concert. Stravinsky wrote to him on April 26: "I of course understand the problem of the small seating in the Scuola di San Rocco, but I understood it last September when I started to compose *Threni*. In spite of the large size of the ensemble, the music is chamber music. . . . The concert could be changed to consist only of *Threni*, which would be played twice with a different audience each time." On May 1, Stravinsky wrote to Rolf Liebermann in Hamburg apropos the *Oedipus Rex* Speaker, who was to have been Vittorio di Sica: "Unless he can agree to commit himself now, I think I had better eliminate the Speaker entirely (which maybe I prefer because the text is rather

159

pompous . . .). We would play only the last of the fanfares for four trumpets, just before the end, and then continue!'' On September 19, at a concert in La Fenice, Stravinsky conducted the orchestra of the Norddeutscher Rundfunk in *Oedipus* and *Sacre* (with the 1943 *Danse sacrale*).

By May 1958, the phlebotomy that had ''contained'' Stravinsky's polycythemia for a year and a half was proving to be an ineffective treatment. On June 7, he wrote to his sons: ''I have just returned from the hospital and I feel very well after the two blood transfusions and the seven days of true rest. My blood count, very low after the hemorrhage three weeks ago, is normal. The red corpuscles are a little higher than 4 million, the hemoglobin is 82 and the hematocrit 40. These levels will not last for long, however, and in three weeks my doctor will give me the first pill of radiophosphate, the effects of which manifest themselves only three months later. . . . As for the ulcer in the duodenum, I must swallow a medication every hour of the day for three months! Not very amusing, but on the other hand, I can eat and drink as I wish. The doctors find that my duodenal ulcers—this is the third time in a decade—are a direct consequence of the condition of my blood, which is much too rich. Perhaps this is flattering, but it is also dangerous.'' On June 16, at Royce Hall, U.C.L.A., Stravinsky conducted *Mavra* and *The Faun and the Shepherdess* as part of the Los Angeles Music Festival. On June 20, he proudly attended an exhibition of his wife's paintings at the Comara Gallery. On July 20, the Stravinskys left for New York, and on July 29 sailed for Genoa on the *Cristoforo Colombo*. After two days (August 7 and 8) at the Hotel Savoy in Genoa, they drove to Venice via Piacenza and Cremona. On September 10, 1958, Lawrence Morton wrote to Mrs. Stravinsky from Los Angeles: ''Madame, you will of course worry. But you will also be beautiful and a little pale. But when the performance is over and you have helped the maestro into dry clothes, then you will be very gay, you will drink, you will love Venice more than ever, and you will get an idea for a wonderful painting.''

161

Stravinsky conducted *Threni* in Hamburg on
October 13, 1958, and on the 14th he and
his wife drove to Baden-Baden, remaining
until the 17th, when they went to
Donaueschingen. After attending a concert
there on the 19th, they drove to Zürich,
accompanied by Pierre Suvchinsky and
Baroness Hansi Lambert. On October 20, the
Stravinskys took the train to Florence (Grand
Hotel). He conducted rehearsals there on the
23rd, 24th, 25th, 26th, and 27th (the date of his
first concert). On the 28th, 29th, and 30th, he
rehearsed for a second concert (30th), then
went to Venice by car, lunching on the way in
Bologna. The Stravinskys entered Venice at
the moment when the bells of the city began
celebrating the elevation of the Patriarch to
the tiara as John XXIII. The Stravinskys

76

departed on the night train to Vienna, arriving
in the Austrian capital on All Saints Day.

On November 2, 3, and 4, Stravinsky
rehearsed *Oedipus Rex* at the Vienna State
Opera, conducting a performance there on
the 4th. On the 5th, 6th, and 7th, he rehearsed
for a Vienna concert, and on the 8th left on the
night train for Paris, where Suvchinsky,
François-Michel, and Boulez taxied the
Stravinskys from the station to the Berkeley
Hotel. Rehearsals followed daily, including
one on November 14, the morning of
Stravinsky's concert. The Stravinskys went
from Paris to Rome, where, on the 26th, the
new Pope sent for the composer. On the 27th,
he conducted the Accademia Filarmonica
Romana at the Teatro Eliseo. On the 28th, the
Stravinskys left Rome for Paris, where they

rested on the 29th at the Berkeley Hotel, dined
with Suzanne Tézenas, and took the night train
for London, arriving (Claridge's) at 9.30 a.m.
on the 30th. On December 4, they attended a
party in their honor at Faber & Faber, and on
the 5th, a luncheon at the Connaught given by
David Astor. On December 14, they were in
Southampton boarding the S.S. *Liberté* for
New York, where they arrived (Gladstone
Hotel) on December 19.

161 *January 2, 1959.* Metropolitan Museum of
Art, New York. With Milton Babbitt, at a
rehearsal of *Threni*.

162 *January 2, 1959.* Metropolitan Museum of
Art. Coaching the singers in *Threni*.

THRENI

1) Venezia
2) Svizzera
3) Hamburos
   et, hilas, Paris
4) American premiere
   in NY, Jan. 4/59
   R. Craft conductors

164

164 *March 1959*. 1260 North Wetherly Drive. Reading *Conversations with Stravinsky*. Photograph from the *San Francisco Examiner*.

165 *March 30, 1959*. With U.S. Cultural Attaché, William Morris, in Tay Tay, the Philippines. The Stravinskys drove from here to a lodge overlooking Lake Taal. That night and the next they dined with Ambassador and Mrs. Bohlen in their residence. On April 1, the Stravinskys flew to Hong Kong (Repulse Bay Hotel).

166 On March 25, 1959, the Stravinskys flew from Los Angeles to Honolulu (Princess Kaiulani Hotel) and the next day toured Oahu Island (below). On the 28th, they left for Manila, arriving there at 5 a.m. on the 30th.

167 *April 1959*. Tokyo.

168 *April 2, 1959.* Hong Kong. Stravinsky
riding in a rickshaw.

169 *April 1959.* Tokyo. Vera Stravinsky at the
exhibition of her paintings.

170, 171, 172 *April 6, 1959.* Tokyo.

JAPAN TIMES,

MONDAY, APRIL 6, 1959

170

171

172

Our arrival
from HongKong
Airport Tokyo
April 6/59

173

174

175

176

173 *April 21, 1959.* Kobe. Lunch at the home of Michi Muriyama.

174, 175, 176 *May 6, 1959.* At the home of Yakichiro Suma, with his family and Hans Popper, whom the Stravinskys had first met in Vienna in November 1958.

Stravinsky conducted three concerts in Japan: Osaka, May 1, and Tokyo, May 3 and 7, but his rehearsal schedule obliged him to make two trips to the former city. Stravinsky was fascinated by Noh, Gagaku, and Kabuki, and he liked the Japanese landscape, at least at Hakone (April 9) and Lake Biwa (April 14). The latter part of his stay in Japan (from April 17) was enlivened by the presence of Nicolas Nabokov.

HOME WITH HONORS—Composer Igor Stravinsky and his wife return to Los Angeles via the SAS polar route. Tuesday night he conducted the Royal Danish Orchestra in Copenhagen, where he received the $7,000 Sonning prize. King Frederik was there.

177

180 *October 14, 1959.* Paestum. On October 12, Stravinsky and I flew from Treviso to Ciampino (Rome), where we were met by Eugene Berman and Robert Bright, the photographer. We drove with them to Sperlonga, to see the excavations, and Naples (Excelsior Hotel). On the 13th, we drove to Gesualdo, where Bright made photographs. On October 15, 16 and 17, I conducted two rehearsals daily at the Teatro San Carlo for a concert there on the 18th. (Between rehearsals, we visited Benevento and the towns of the Campania.) The Naples program included *Apollo* and *Pulcinella*, conducted by Stravinsky, and Berg's Three Pieces for Orchestra, conducted by me. After the concert, which began at 6.15 p.m., we dined at Hans Werner Henze's, then left on the midnight train for Bologna.

178

177 *May 27, 1959.* Los Angeles airport. Home from Copenhagen.

178, 179 *June 1959.* With Christopher Isherwood in front of his home in Santa Monica.

179

181

182

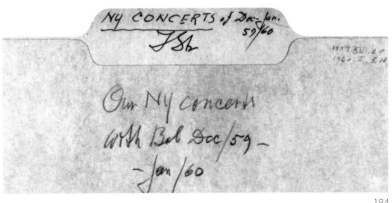

Rehearsal for the Dec 20th 1959
Concert in Town Hall, New York

NY CONCERTS of Dec–Jan.
59/60
1959 XII 20
1960. I. 3, 10

Our NY concerts
with Bob Dec/59 –
– Jan/60

181 *October 14, 1959*. Paestum.

182 *October 1959*. Naples.

183 *December 16, 1959*. Rehearsal of the pianists for *Les Noces*. L. to r: Lukas Foss, Samuel Barber, Aaron Copland, Roger Sessions. The tenor, Loren Driscoll, is seated at the center.

183

184

185 *October 13, 1959.* In the courtyard of the castle at Gesualdo.

187

188

189

187 *June 29, 1959.* The Stravinskys leave their train at Lamy (Santa Fe).

188 *July 21, 1958.* Waiting with Paul Horgan and Miranda Levy for the Stravinskys' train from Los Angeles to New York. Miranda Levy was a close friend of both Stravinskys from 1950 until their deaths. The poet Witter Bynner wrote to her on February 18, 1954: ''You should have seen—and felt—Stravinsky guiding me, his arm in mine, down the path from his house to the car, loving my blindness. He had said, 'They liked my early work, and now they like only my early work. They liked me too soon. But I know that I like what I do now—and they will be liking it sometime, but I like it now. I'm ahead of them. And I will always be ahead of them.'''

189 *July 18, 1960.* Picnic with Paul Horgan at Bandelier National Monument.

190 *July 25, 1961.* Waiting with Paul Horgan and Frank McGee for the Super Chief, which the Stravinskys were to take to Los Angeles.

190

191–194 *June 20, 1960*. Vernissage at the Comara Gallery, Hollywood. (**192**) The woman between the Stravinskys is Mrs. Sol Babitz.

195 *October 20, 1960*. Venice. Birthday card from Vera Stravinsky.

191

192

193

194

196

197

198

196 *January 1960*. New York. Gladstone Hotel. Photograph by Claudio Spies.

197 *August 29, 1960*. Buenos Aires. Press conference.

198 *August 29, 1960*. San Isidro, Buenos Aires. Angelica Ocampo (standing), Victoria Ocampo (seated).

199 *August 18, 1960*. Pachacamac, Peru.

200 *August 29, 1960*. San Isidro.

200

201 *January 1961.* Stravinsky had known Salvador Dali since the 1920s and once rode with him in a train between Madrid and Barcelona. I had seen the two men together only once, on March 5, 1953, the day that the news of Stalin's death was released. Dali had invited the Stravinskys to lunch at the St. Regis Hotel; or, rather, Edward James, who had a vast collection of Dalis, had arranged the lunch, and though Dali was supposed to be the host, after glancing at the check, he quickly passed it to James. In January 1961, Dali, residing on the same floor as the Stravinskys in the St. Regis, was trying to convince the composer to collaborate with him on a lucrative theatrical venture. After two futile attempts to reach an agreement, Dali inscribed the fly-leaf of the new book of

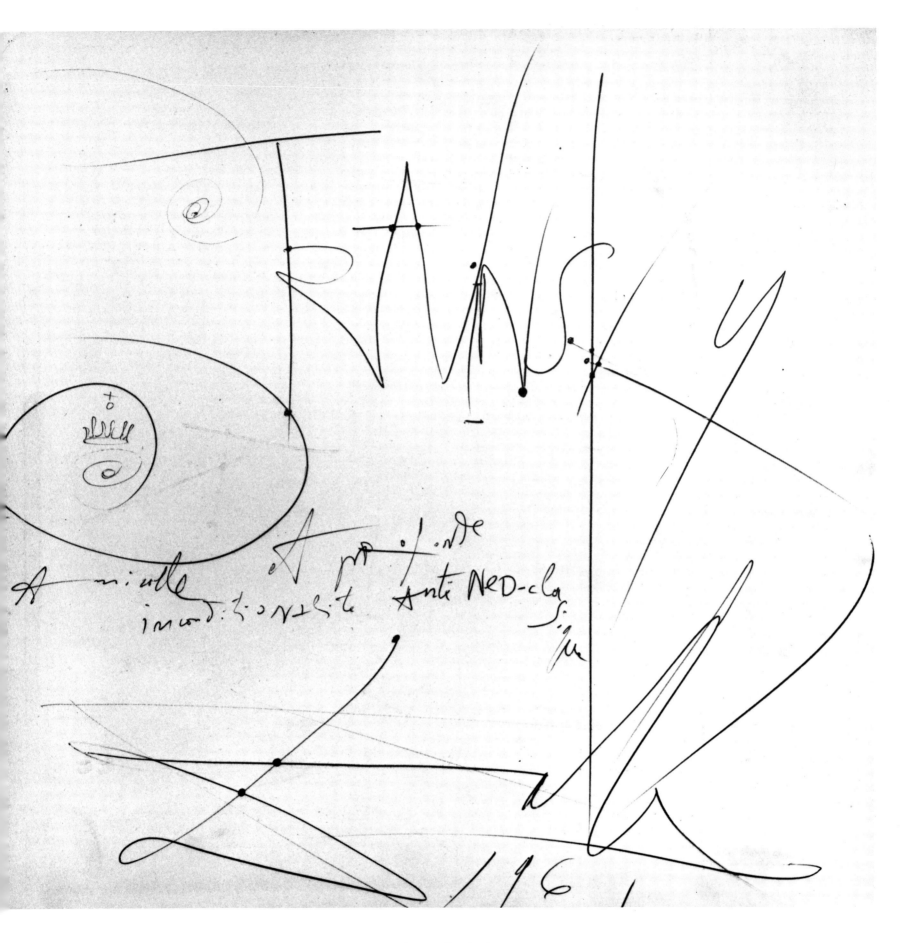

his art for Stravinsky: "*Hommage très Amicalle* [sic] *et profonde*[,] *Dali*[,] *Inconditionaliste*[,] *Anti Neo-Clasique* [sic]." Stravinsky considered the dedication an insult and gave the drawing to me. Paul Horgan wrote (*Encounters with Stravinsky*): "Dali, whose suite was further down the corridor than the Stravinskys', whistled *Frère Jacques* (or perhaps it was Mahler's First Symphony) between the elevator and his rooms as a signal to his wife that he was returning. Since the insulation was very poor and Stravinsky heard this, his annoyance with the painter was further aggravated." The drawing was executed with amazing speed and virtuosity.

202

204

203

202, 203 *July 29, 1961.* Santa Fe. Exhibition of paintings and rugs by Vera Stravinsky. With Victor Babin and Vitya Vronsky.

204 *April 1961.* Mexico City. Exhibition of Vera Stravinsky's paintings at the Galleria Diana.

205 *June 1961.* Beverly Hills. At the home of Bart Lytton, during a party for the Los Angeles Music Festival. Also present was a group of Soviet musicians who, a few days later, invited Stravinsky to visit the U.S.S.R. in 1962.

Three Texts recitation, and chorus
for solo voices, ~~chorus texts~~

Notes: Section ① could be cut entirely, especially if you don't want a chorus — I had thought of it as a choral piece of 4 minutes or so. The lines in parenthesis could be spoken if you wish to mix singing & speech — at any rate they can be uttered at the same time. This might be a good text for divided chorus or double chorus the first 2 lines sung by one chorus while the 3rd line is spoken by the other chorus; the and OUR GOD line by tutti, etc. [The texts are from Romans 8, 24, + 2 different places in Hebrews.]

② is a short Passion, not a gospel + therefore not part of a service, very useful for the purpose of a cantata of this sort. I know of no musical setting, which is strange because it is the most concise as well as the most touching story I know in the Bible outside of the Gospels. (at the end "he fell asleep" is surely as poignant and simple and as moving as any description in the whole Christian Testament.)

There are many possibilities of telling this story — by different voices, a narrator, etc. or even alto since Stephen might be a tenor

and I have grouped the text to show possible divisions, though there can be many more. In any case, the narrators part is a large one, + the trick will be to find a way of doing this finding a recitative style; this piece should take 15 minutes.

The last piece ③, the prayer — follows very naturally the death of Stephen — and though it is not Biblical, the style is very close. The red line shows a good division — an idea that perhaps the first part could be sung by a solo voice contralto, or two solo voices in canon, + the second part by the chorus. [The word 'blessed' has two syllables.]

As the Canticum + Threni were Old Testament (largely) Latin, formal, large, choral, so this as text and idea anyway, is New Testament personal intimate and the middle part, Stephen, suggests solo voices more. IT should all be in the vernacular (English), as the New Testament should be + as the dramatic newness of Stephen's stoning must be — also, to distinguish the newness of Christianity from the Old Testament.

206, 207 These thoughts concerning *A Sermon, a Narrative, and a Prayer* are the source for the program note, *Meine neue Kantate*, that Stravinsky sent to Paul Sacher, August 7, 1961. As this photocopy shows, Stravinsky changed the subtitle—the word "recitation" is in his hand—and underlined my phrase (lines 2, 3 of right column) "though there can be many more." Press coverage at the premiere, Basel, February 22, 1962, was extensive, but the only review that Stravinsky seems to have noticed was the one in *Le Monde* (Paris), February 25–26, titled "Création à Bâle." He wrote over this: "Création pas très bien reçue (comme d'habitude) par un critique très élogieux (comme d'habitude) pour l'exécutant." Stravinsky also underscored and questioned the critic's observation that the piece does not disdain description, since it "evokes the disputes in the synagogue by means of an ironic counterpoint of bassoon and oboe." Stravinsky drew larger question marks next to the *Monde* critic's statement that, surprisingly, the score "attains the intensity and the grandeur of a work such as the *Canti di Prigioniera* by Dallapiccola."

The text of the ST. Stephen — this is very much abbreviated and cut but it is complete enough for our purpose, + the progress from beginning to end in so short a span is amazing.

The timing of the whole seems to suggest 20 minutes though possibly less (but Basel would certainly not complain if they had 18 min.)

O my God, if it bee thy pleasure to cut me off before night, yet make me, my gracious Shepheard, for one of thy Lambs, to whom thou wilt say, "Come you blessed," and clothe mee in a white robe of righteousness, that I may be one of those singers, who shall sing to thee alleluia.

from *Foure Birds of Noahs Arke*
by Thomas Dekker

Maestro just listened!

COMPOSER and conductor Igor → Stravinsky, right, just sat and listened as his associate, Robert Craft, above, conducted the 82-piece Victorian Symphony Orchestra at a Melbourne Town Hall rehearsal yesterday.

Stravinsky's one and only Melbourne concert will be held at the Palais Theatre, St. Kilda, tonight.

Yesterday the 79-year-old maestro sat near the rostrum, beating time and occasionally jumping up to have a quick word with Craft.

209

208, 209, 210 *November 23, 1961.* Rehearsal for a concert in Sidney, Australia, on November 24, 1961. Stravinsky conducted the Symphony in Three Movements. (**210**) The Kahan cartoon was drawn at this rehearsal.

210

211–214 Unpublished version for ten wind instruments of the ''Tango'' (No 8) from *The Five Fingers* (1921). Arranged in Hollywood, December 1961, and performed in Mexico City the same month.

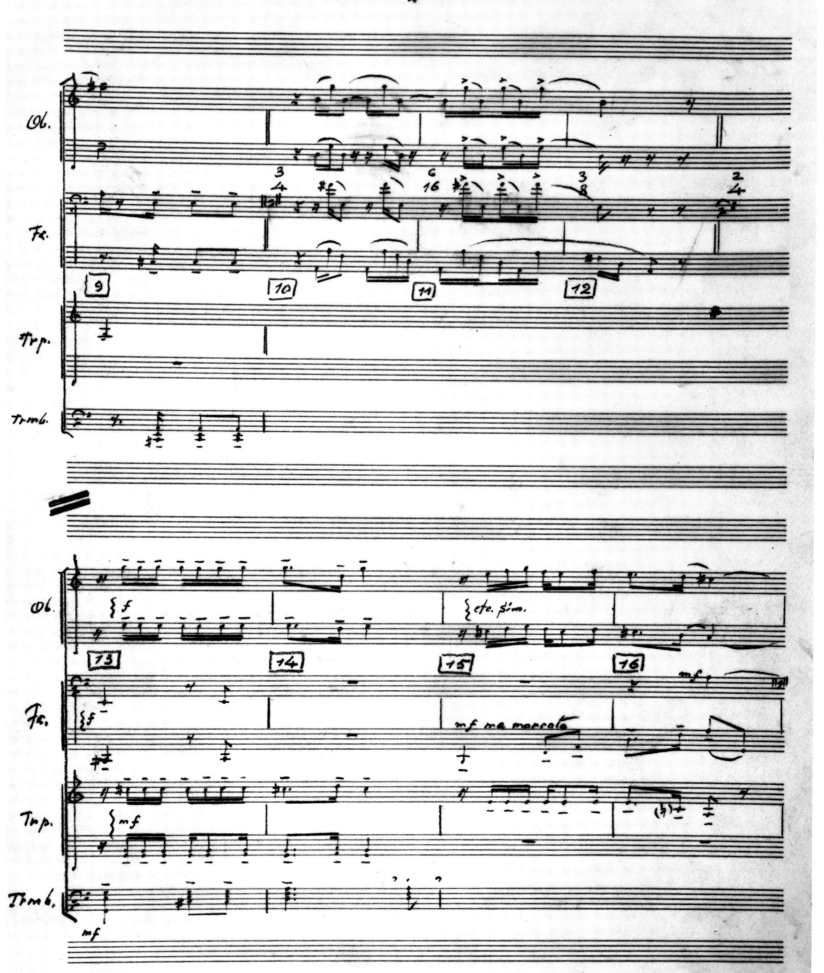

— 3 —

213

105

for you, Bob
JSt

Igor Stravinsky

The Flood

215

216

216, 217 *March 31, 1962.* Between and during recording sessions of *The Flood*.

218

218 *January 19, 1962.* After a rehearsal of *Oedipus Rex*, Washington, D.C. Drawing by René Bouché.

217

219, 220 *May 17, 1962.* Arrival at Johannesburg. Photo from the *Sunday Express.* The late Anton Hartman was music director of the South African Broadcasting Company. On May 23, the *Rand Daily Mail* published this interview:

. . . Mrs. Vera Stravinsky, wife of the world's most celebrated composer, is asked in every country she visits: "What is it like to live with a genius?" and this quiet-spoken, friendly and calm woman, 5 ft. 8 inches tall, with hazel eyes and auburn hair, tinted to leave two white streaks sweeping back from her forehead, has a habit of catching this question and tossing it back to you. "What would *you* do if you lived with a genius?" With a warm smile, she continues: "After all, we are surrounded by geniuses. Our two closest friends, Aldous Huxley and Christopher Isherwood, are both geniuses. Maybe I am a genius too, no?"

[In 1940] the Stravinskys went to live in Los Angeles. "Ah, but Hollywood was marvelous in those days," sighed Mrs. Stravinsky. ". . . All our friends—refugees—were there too. Now life starts to be very lonesome. Everyone travels and now Hollywood is empty. So we travel too. Particularly this year, when my husband will be 80. We have a large house and garden—but I am not allowed to grow vegetables or keep chickens. During the war, yes, but now, no. Our house, it is so full—we cannot move. There are books everywhere. . . . I think we have more than 5,000 books. They are on the chairs, on the tables, on the floor. Twice we enlarged our house and still there is no room." She gestured towards an untidy pile of books in the hotel room. "We travel with books, too many books."

". . . I have many little hobbies," she replied to a question, then, waving a beringed hand, "but my husband, no! He has no hobbies, only music. Music is his whole life. I like to collect paintings, young painters mostly. . . . Picasso is a friend from our Paris days, but it is many years since we have seen him. Like us, he hates the big party, he likes to meet in a café and talk. Oh, those big receptions after concerts are awful!"

"I am a good cook," she nodded emphatically in reply to another question. "Stravinsky's favorite dish is *caviare au blini* . . . you know, those Russian pancakes with caviar and cream. And [smoked] salmon he likes too. . . . He will drink only Scotch or champagne."

221 *September 1962.* On a Moscow television program.

219

220

222

223

224

110

222–226 Throughout the last twenty-five years
of his life, Stravinsky was in the habit of
cupping his left ear while rehearsing or
listening to rehearsals and performances.
(**222**) *1953*. New York. Listening to playbacks.
(**223**) *1947*. New York. (**224**) *1956*. (**225**)
January 1957. Rehearsing the New York
Philharmonic. (**226**) *August 1970*. Evian.
Photograph by Snowdon.

226

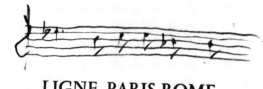

LIGNE PARIS-ROME
PAR CARAVELLE

227

228

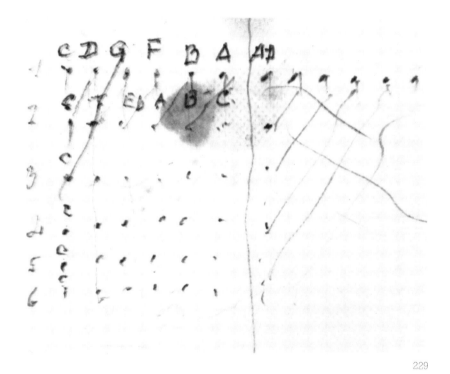

229

227, 228 *October 11, 1962.* In flight between
Paris and Rome. (**228**) A twelve-tone series
written on the Air France menu in response to
the pilot's request for an autograph. (He
forgot to take it, but I did not.)

229 This incomplete series, sketched on a
used paper napkin during another flight,
reveals that Stravinsky had intended to use
the rotations of the beta hexachord in two
(criss-crossing) directions.

230 *1960.* 1260 North Wetherly Drive.

230

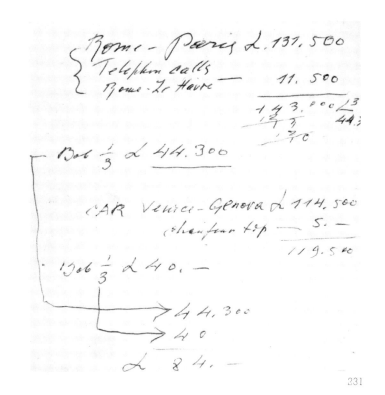

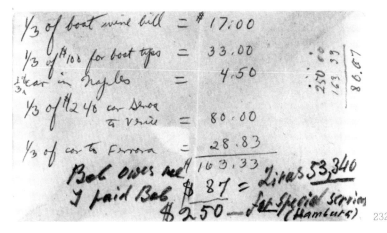

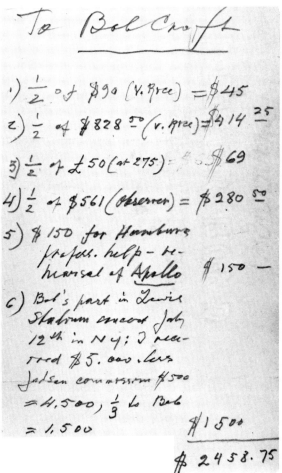

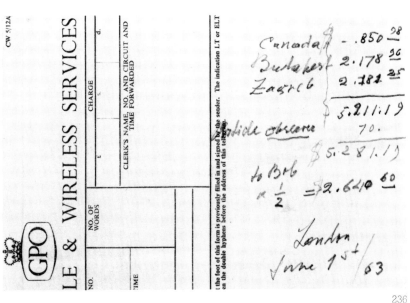

231–236 The statements of account date from, clockwise (from top left): September 1958 (Venice), July 1962 (New York), May 1962 (New York), April 1959 (Osaka), June 1963 (London).

237 *May 5, 1963.* Hamburg. Leaving for a concert in Budapest.

238, 239 *May 29, 1963.* Albert Hall, London. Applauding Pierre Monteux's fiftieth-anniversary performance of *Le Sacre du printemps.*

238

240 *November 20, 1963*. New York. Stravinsky's drawing on a Carnegie Hall program.

241 *1963*. 1260 North Wetherly Drive.

242

243

244

242 *June 1, 1963.* Stravinsky's design for a gold medallion as a gift for his daughter-in-law, Denise (Mrs. Theodore) Stravinsky. The music is the beginning of the ''Te Deum'' from *The Flood.*

243, 244 *October 20, 1963.*

245 *June 14, 1964.* Stravinsky wrote this comparison of the first themes of his Symphony in C and Tchaikovsky's First Symphony on a paper napkin in flight between Denver and New York. On June 13, he had conducted the second half of a concert in a hall in Denver, an event that had been rained-out from Red Rocks. The Stravinskys had flown to Denver, July 11, and stayed in the Brown Palace Hotel.

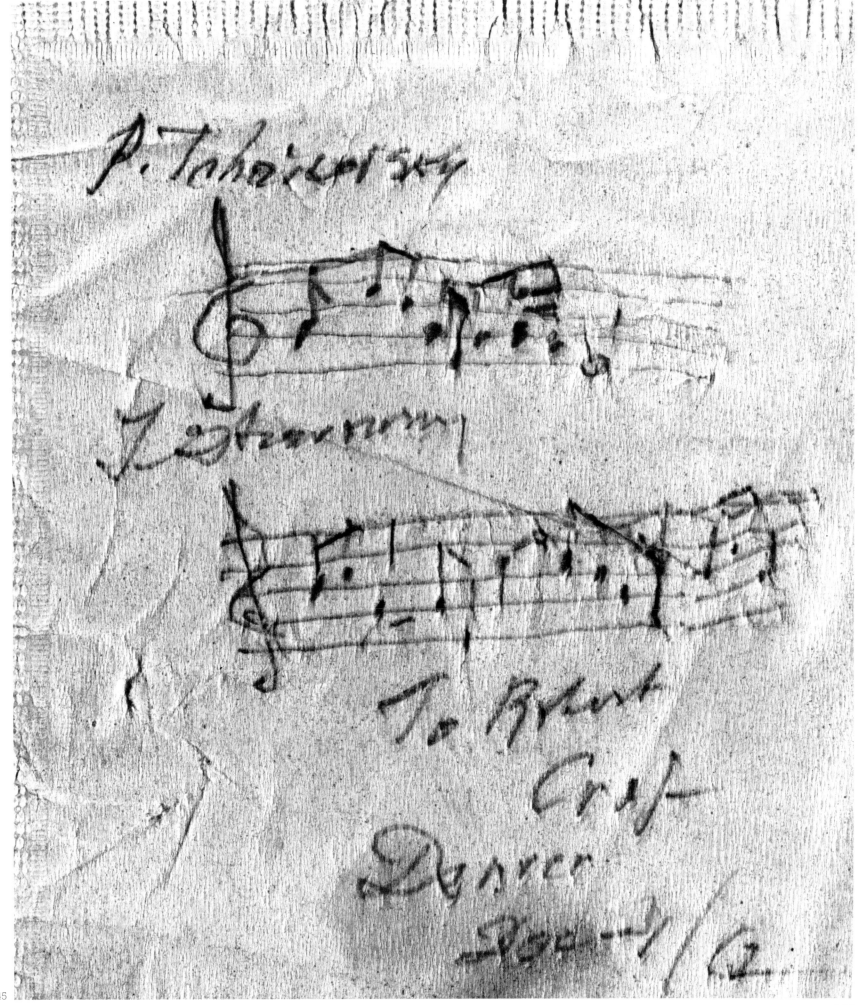

246

247

247, 248 The music example in Stravinsky's first draft of a program note for *Abraham and Isaac* reveals part of his technique of composition. (**248**) The pertinent sentence reads: "Some stressed octaves and fifths and doubled intervals which could be found in this score shouldn't contradict the serial basis of the composition; [their] origin . . . lies not in an horizontal contrapunctical accord of different voices but in a vertical simultaneous clang (sounding?) of several notes belonging to a certain number of forms [rotations] played together." The example that he gives, however, is not from *Abraham and Isaac* but from the Variations—the alpha hexachords of the series in its original form. The notes in the frame are found at the first beat of measure 133. The six verticals to the left of the frame are the notes in the chord in measure 132, the six to the right form the chord in the second beat of measure 133.

248

249

249 *September 1962.* Jerusalem. Receiving a medal from Theodore Kollek in the home of President Ben Zvi (right).

251 *September 1962.* The Mann Auditorium, Tel Aviv.

איגור סטרווינסקי

רוברט קרפט

THE ISRAEL FESTIVAL, 1964

July 12 — August 31, 1964

KOL ISRAEL SYMPHONY ORCHESTRA
HAIFA CITY SYMPHONY ORCHESTRA

Preparation of Orchestras: MENDI RODAN

Conductors: **IGOR STRAVINSKY**

ROBERT CRAFT

250

251

252, 253 *August 26, 1964.* New York. Photographs by Robert Cato.

254 *October 1964.* The questions concerning *Orpheus* were prompted by a request from Columbia Records for program notes.

252

253

URGENT
you can not complain
[initials]

Oct 3/64

Orpheus

1. The subject was whose idea?   Balanchine

   " commission came when?   1946

   When did you start to compose?   1946

2. When did Balanchine come to Los A. to discuss it (1946?) Yes

   How did you plan the action together?   Together

   Is the ordering of the plot jointly yours + Balanchine's   Together

   Whose version of the myth did you follow (the titles   all the dictionaries French
   were composed by whom?)   (Ovid?)   I used Ovid
   by myself
   after the dictionaries

3. Did you have any ~~concept~~ mural conceptions for the staging   He Abs-
   ~~costumes~~   Not
   any ~~costumes~~ ideas?   when composing   What about the masks?   Noguchi, I think

   Noguchi was Kirstein's idea?   I think so

   How did you find the staging in comparison to your
   conception?   I liked, when I saw at Noguchi's studio
   how small theater images the (theatrical sketch)

4. Did Balanchine offer any ~~precisions~~ (specifications) as to the lengths of
   the ~~individual~~ individual dances?   More or less, but we
   decided it ~~together~~ than

5. What music by other composers most attracted you
   at the time and were there any "influences"?
        nobody's   I didn't and don't
                         for it
6. *Orpheus* is what I may be prefer today ~~of~~ all my,
   So called, neo-classical period.

254   123

255

255 *1964*. Toronto. Photograph by Amletto Lorenzini.

256 *September 1957*. In St. Mark's, Venice. Photograph by Gjon Mili.

257 The 80th birthday greeting by Joan Miró was made in June 1962.

Pour Universtire,

Bon

cher Stravinsky,

Miró. 1962.

127

258 *July 1980*. Lake Mohonk, New York, with Edwin Allen.

259 *September 1981*. London. With Mme Lucia Davidova.

260 *January 1982*. Fort Lauderdale Airport.

261

261–264 The writings, the accounting, and the photograph on this page all date from 1964.

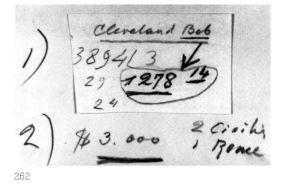

262

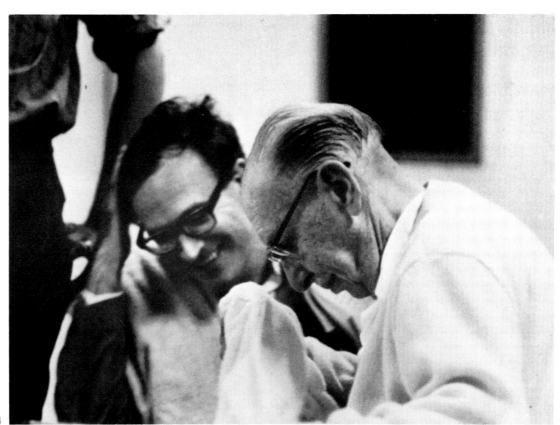

263

264

129

Maestro arrives

FAMED COMPOSER and conductor Igor Stravinsky, shown with Mrs. Stravinsky, has arrived in town to rehearse for his forthcoming Vancouver Festival concerts with the Vancouver Symphony Orchestra. They will be held next Monday, Tuesday. 265

to you, dear Bob
who performed Saturday
April 12/65 my VARIATIONS
for the first time

266

265 *July 9, 1965*. Vancouver. Stravinsky
conducted the Vancouver Symphony
Orchestra on July 12 and 13. Photograph from
The Province. Interview from *The Vancouver
Sun*, July 12, 1965:

. . . The charming Madame Igor Stravinsky,
interviewed Saturday at the Bayshore, . . . was a
lovely lesson in the art of being a woman. . . . Her
eyes, her hands and her lilting voice enhanced
every word. She knew it. I knew it. And we both
enjoyed it.

Asked about her husband, here to conduct
concerts for the Vancouver Festival tonight and
Tuesday at the Queen Elizabeth Theater, she
explained that he is a "very spoiled man. . . . Igor
is so spoiled that maybe he could make tea—
maybe." . . . This wife who obviously adores
spoiling her husband and being spoiled in turn by
him, would not admit to his reputation for
temperament. "He is capricious. We are both
capricious and make little scenes for maybe five
minutes. . . . He needs me now because he is 83

and sometines he tires. When I suggest that he
should stay at home for a year and do some
composing—he has many commissions—he is
annoyed and asks if [I think] he can no longer
conduct. . . ."

After his concerts here, the Stravinskys are
returning home. They have just completed a tour of
Europe and a concert in Chicago. "It was a
wonderful tour and we were invited by the Pope to
hear an orchestra play Igor's *Symphony of Psalms*.
We were invited to be seated next to the Pope but
the Vatican is not like a subway. 'Next to the Pope'
means across the room from where he sits in his
golden chair." Madame Stravinsky was as pleasant
to see as to hear. The overworked word "chic"
could honestly be used to describe her appearance.
She wore a deceptively simple black dress with
pearls and an emerald pin. Her auburn hair has a
wing of white at the temple and at the back she
wore a soft velvet bow of American beauty rose.

"It is good to gossip with a woman. It happens so
seldom because always the conversation seems to
be music. I like to talk about clothes and cooking

and the country. I was brought up on what you
would call a ranch. It was a country estate near St.
Petersburg. I did not see a city until I was 12 and I
am still always happy to see a cow or a horse. We
have bought a new home and in it is a big studio for
me." Almost shyly she revealed that she paints—has
had numerous shows both on this continent and in
Europe. Asked if she paints under her own name,
Vera de Bosset, she answered, "No. My friends told
me it would help my career if I used my married
name, Vera Stravinsky. But it hasn't. As soon as
[people] see that name, they want to know about my
husband—not me." But a happy little shrug and a
waft of the hand showed how little she minds.
"After all, my husband is a *great* artist."

266 Stravinsky wrote this copy of the series of
his Variations in flight between Chicago and
New York, April 14, 1965.

267 *October 26, 1965*. Hollywood. Recording
session.

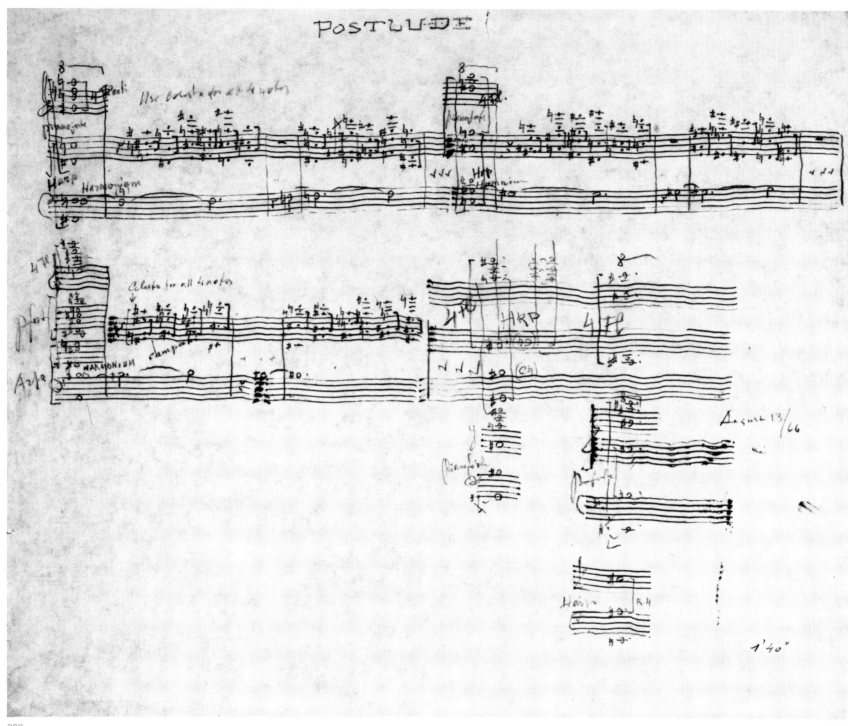

POSTLUDE

268 First draft score of the Postlude from the *Requiem Canticles*, dated August 13, 1966, and timed to 1 minute and 40 seconds. Some of the chords combine pitches from both of the work's twelve-tone series. The harmonies of the first four measures are constructed from the original order of series II (F, C, B, A, A sharp, D sharp, C sharp, G sharp, F sharp, E, G, D). The chord in the sixth measure is built from both the original and retrograde forms of the hexachords of series II. The six chords in the next measure combine original and retrograde components of both series, as follows (upper to lower lines): series II,

retrograde; series I, retrograde; series II, original; series I, original. (The pitches of series I, original, are: F, G, D sharp, E, F sharp, C sharp, B, C, D, A, G sharp, A sharp.) The harmonies in the next two measures derive from the same orders, except that only the beta hexachords are used. The eight-pitch chord in measure eleven, and the chords in measures 12–14, derive from the original form of series I, alpha hexachord, and the inverted form of series I, beta hexachord. The final two chords, found in the same sketch-page as the first chord of the Postlude, with Stravinsky's note,

"beginning and finishing," are derived from series I. The five pitches of the penultimate chord are from the original form. The four pitches of the final chord are from the inverted form, both gamma and beta pitch-collections. The script above the staves reads "Use celesta for all 4 notes."

269 *November 1965*. Hollywood. Sketch for the beginning of the *Requiem Canticles*. Stravinsky was reading *Ulysses* at the time.

270 *Spring 1966*. 1218 North Wetherly Drive.

132

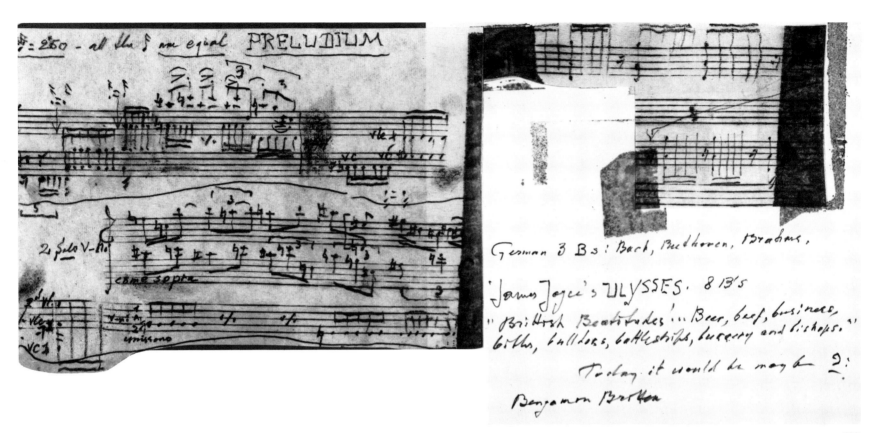

German 3 B's: Bach, Beethoven, Brahms.

'James Joyce's ULYSSES. 8 B's

'British Beatitudes' ... Beer, beef, business,
bibles, bulldogs, battleships, buggery and bishops."

Today it would be maybe 2:

Benjamin Britten

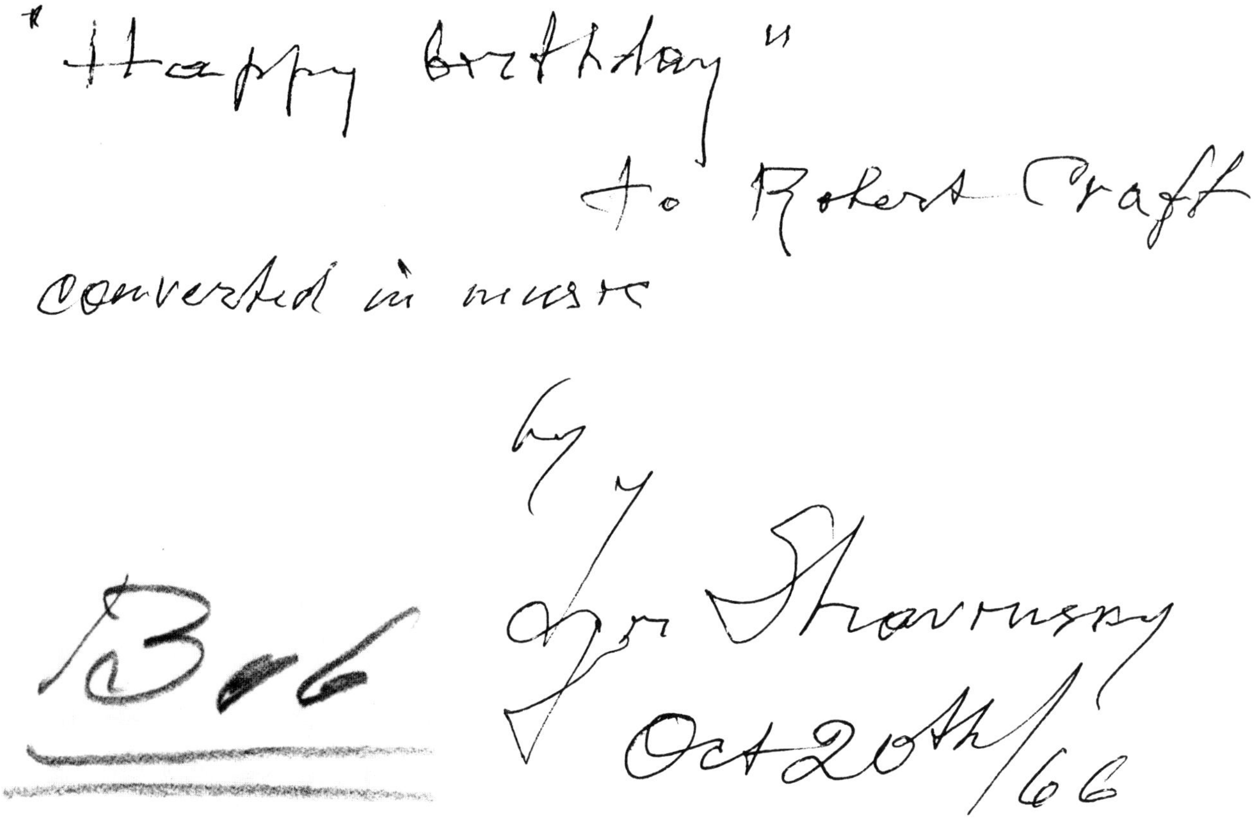
"Happy Birthday"
to Robert Craft
converted in music
by
Igor Stravinsky
Oct 20th/66
Bob

271

272

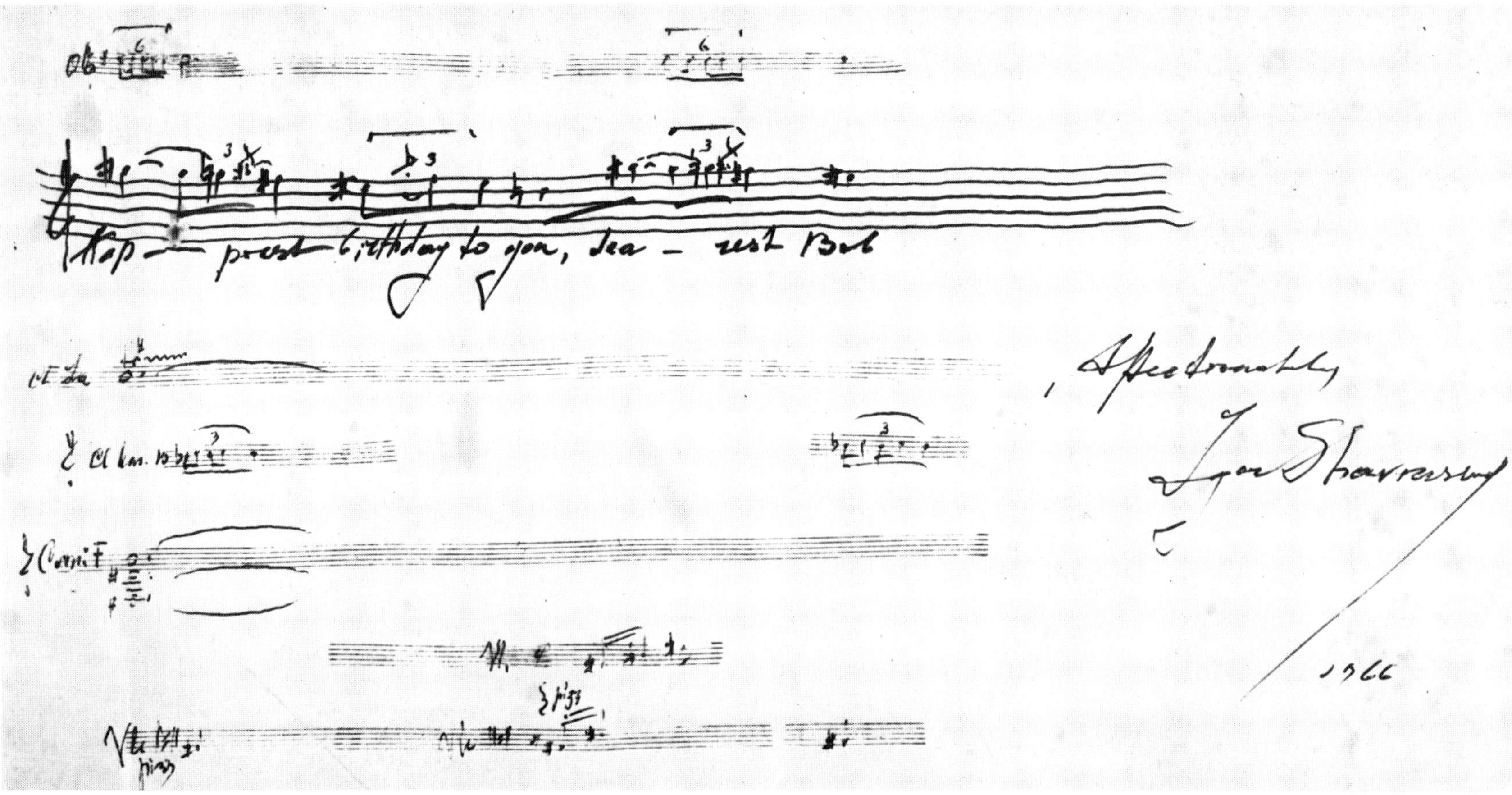
Hap — piest birthday to you, dea — rest Bob
Affectionately
Igor Stravinsky
1966

273

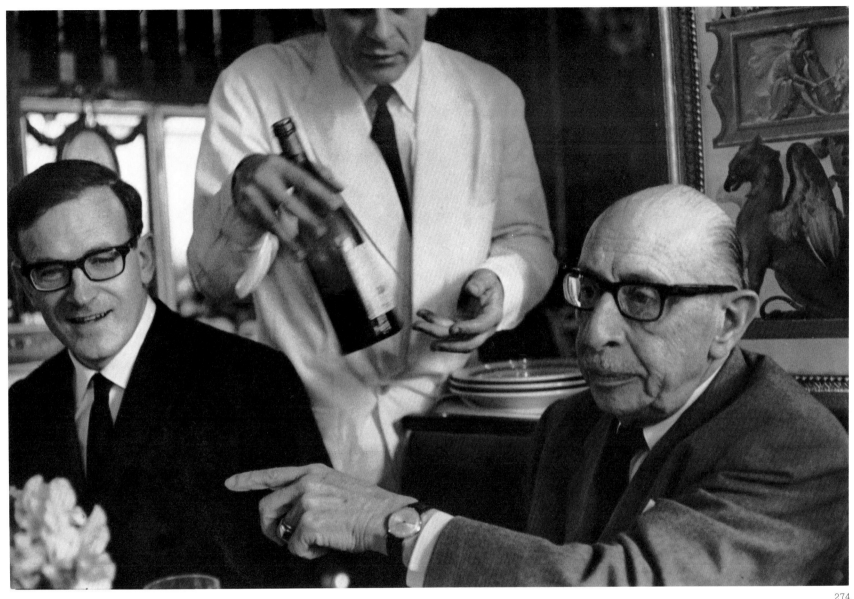

274

272, 273 *October 20, 1966*. The music is from *Le Sacre du printemps*.

274 *June 6, 1966*. Paris. The Grand Vefour. Photograph by Henri Cartier-Bresson.

Luncheon by the Paris Bureau of *The New York Times*. In April 1966, *The Times* commissioned me to write two pieces, one *about* Stravinsky, for the Sunday, June 26, music page, one *by* him for the magazine section. The deadlines were long before the publication dates, and I finished the first article, "A Master at Work," before the end of April, and sent it to my agent, Miss Rice. On May 1, I received a note from her: "I just had an ecstatic phone call from *The New York*

Times. Seymour Peck is delighted with your piece and asked me to tell both you and Mr. Stravinsky." On May 14, The New York Times Company issued a check in my name attached to a voucher describing the sum as payment for "A Master at Work." On May 29, I wrote Miss Rice from Europe, saying that I wished to make revisions. On June 11, I wrote again: "The *Times*'s Paris Bureau took the revised manuscript to retype it, but kept it for four days after which it was still loaded with errors. . . ." On June 14, I informed Miss Rice that "Mr. Stravinsky has a cold and we are not going to Strasbourg. This means that I have to change the *Times* article. What I describe in it took place ten months ago, in accordance with

Mr. Peck's request for characteristics and idiosyncrasies, and general and habitual behavior; dates and places were understood to be merely incidental. This, it seems, is standard newspaper practice, and not only with obits. Nevertheless, the passage should be cut." Miss Rice responded on June 17: "In regard to your piece for Seymour Peck: as it happens they are publishing it this Sunday and had already gone to press. However, they managed to cut out the Strasbourg part in all but the first edition, which will not be distributed in New York, but only in a few outlandish places." This was my first and last experience with before-the-event journalism.

276

275 *1964.* Toronto. Photograph by Amletto Lorenzini.

276, 277, 278 *September 16, 1966.* Louisville.

The Master Listens

Wearing two pairs of eyeglasses, Igor Stravinsky follows the score of his composition, *The Firebird*, at right above, while his assistant, Robert Craft, rehearses the Louisville Orchestra, at the left. At right, Stravinsky in a pensive mood. Stravinsky will be guest conductor of the Louisville Orchestra in a concert of his works at 8:30 tomorrow night in Convention Center. It is the climax of the weeklong Downtown Salutes the Arts. The rehearsal yesterday was at Atherton High School. *September 1966.*

277   278

279

279 *March 1967.* In the library, 1218 North Wetherly Drive. Photograph by Roddy McDowall.

281 *October 1968.* Zürich. Sketch for a three-voice setting of *Otche Nash* (*Pater Noster*).

THE COMPOSER AND MME. STRAVINSKY IN BERKELEY IN 1968
When their romance began in Paris, they were both married to others

280

281

282

282 *December 5, 1969*. New York. Essex House. Photograph by *Time* Magazine.

283 *1968*. 1218 North Wetherly Drive. Photograph by Roddy McDowall.

284, 285 *April 15, 1971*. Venice. Leaving Santi Giovanni e Paolo for San Michele.

283

284

285

286 *March 1978.* London. The Crane Kalman Gallery. With Lady Falkender and David Hockney at the exhibition of Vera Stravinsky's paintings.

287 *September 22, 1982.* San Michele.

286

287

Pictures from Albums of the Past

M. Ravel,
Waglav Nijinski et
sa soeur
Bronislava Nijinska
à Paris sur le balcon de
M. Ravel Av. Carnot en 1914

288 *Spring 1911.* Beaulieu-sur-Mer, with
Diaghilev. Stravinsky's *Petrushka* sketchbooks
and scores are underarm.

289 *June 1912.* ''M. Ravel, Wazlav Nijinski et
sa soeur Bronislava Nijinska à Paris sur le
balcon de M. Ravel Av. Carnot en 1914 [*sic,*
but in fact 1912].'' Photo by Stravinsky.

291

290, 291 *Valse des Fleurs.*

147

293

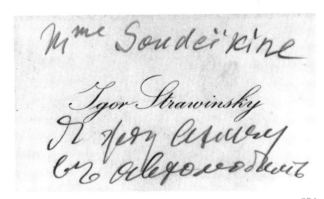

294

292 *February 28, 1926.* Amsterdam.
Concertgebouw. "My rehearsals of the *Sacre*.
Beside me Willem Mengelberg."

293 *January 1927.* Paris. Photo for a driver's
license.

294 *1921.* Paris. Vera Sudeikina's first
memento of her future husband, a calling card
saying that he is waiting in the street in front
of her apartment with an automobile.

295 *1924.* Paris. In Stravinsky's Pleyel Studio.

295

296 *1939*. Paris. Photo by Hoyningen-Huene.

297 *1930*. Amsterdam.

298 *December 8, 1931.* Frankfurt.

APPENDIX

Stravinsky's Medical Diaries

WHILE CONDUCTING THE SYMPHONY IN C in Berlin, October 2, 1956, Stravinsky suffered a thrombosis (basilar stenosis). The medical records that he kept thereafter, the principal autobiographical document in his own hand, reveal that polycythemia, which was diagnosed in London two months later, became the primary concern of his later years. In London, a bloodletting treatment was begun that required hematological analyses every few weeks, an interval that later shrank to a few days and sometimes even hours. In order to compare these blood tests and to follow schedules of medications, chiefly of dosages of anti-coagulants, Stravinsky entered the results in books marked "daily reminders."

On May 18, 1957, Stravinsky wrote to his sons:

In spite of the constant and sometimes powerful numbness, I am in good health, my weight is good, heart good, blood pressure good, and blood less thick than in Europe. The red corpuscles are not yet normal, which means that they accumulate and that I have six million instead of five. In these last weeks, my doctor, Knauer, has given me daily injections of embryonic liver-cells, and he will soon begin a treatment with cardiovascular cells. For the present, he will continue with the weekly bleedings.

On June 3, 1957, Stravinsky wrote to his niece and nephew, Ira and Gania Beliankin: "Happily, my health is good now, and the blood components are in normal proportion to one another and stabilized."

This stability lasted only until May 1958, when Stravinsky was hospitalized suffering from a bleeding duodenal ulcer. After several transfusions at the Cedars of Lebanon Department of Nuclear Medicine (Los Angeles), he was injected with radioactive phosphorus. This was supposed to control the production of the blood, but though experiments with the substance, P-32, had been carried out since 1943, the side-effects and ultimate consequences (leukemia?) were not yet known. For this reason, from November 1962 to September 1970, when the disease disappeared or, at any rate, no longer troubled Stravinsky, his physicians resumed the former method of phlebotomy. Meanwhile, in January 1960, Stravinsky wrote to his friend Pierre Suvchinsky:

Yesterday I saw my doctor, Hans Schiff. . . . He promised, with injections and pills, to change my condition which, to tell the truth, torments me constantly and painfully, so much that I believe in and rejoice at any promise of help. My blood pressure is completely normal, which the doctor considers to be extremely important.

Stravinsky wrote to Suvchinsky again on February 28:

My health is good now. I am in the hands of specialists who have begun taking good care of me. They were waiting for me to settle down a bit, and I am staying here until July, when I will go to Santa Fe for two weeks to conduct *Oedipus* (and Bob *The Rake*). The doctors had to monitor my blood almost daily, which required that I stay here. . . . A week ago I began taking sintrom tablets and shall continue to take them for the rest of my life, to reduce the coagulation of the blood and prevent a repetition of what happened to me in Bologna in October[1] and in London[2] three years ago. Already the daily monitorings of my blood—which will continue for

four months, after which I will have a blood test every three weeks—show good results. The doctors promise that I will be feeling completely different. I want to believe this is true.

On January 30, 1961, Stravinsky wrote to his son Theodore:

I suddenly had a huge black and blue mark on my left knee. Nothing dangerous: this is a frequent side-effect in people who take sintropane, a medication that I have been using for a year to prevent coagulation in the blood. Now my blood and blood pressure are normal, but my right arm and leg always feel very heavy.

Stravinsky's diaries testify to his indomitable physical and moral strength. That a man of his age could spend an hour or two with doctors almost daily, undergoing blood tests, X-rays, and other examinations (axial tomography in July 1969), enduring untold discomforts and fears, and still compose *Agon*, *Threni*, Movements, *A Sermon, a Narrative, and a Prayer*, *Abraham and Isaac*, *The Flood*, the Variations, and the *Requiem Canticles*, is scarcely believable. Moreover, he observed the same medical regimen during his travels, beginning early on the first morning after his arrival in a different city and country. His concert itinerary in 1960–62 would have daunted a much younger man in perfect health. In addition to the blood disease, Stravinsky's susceptibility to colds and influenza was extremely high, and from January 1957 until his death, both his mobility and his capacity to stand and conduct were greatly impeded by a hernia.

The diaries for 1963, 1965, and 1967 are not included here; they could not be located but must have been preserved by William Montapert, Stravinsky's one-time lawyer, or Andre Marion, the composer's son-in-law. These two "business managers" induced Stravinsky to record his tax-deductible expenses—entertainment costs, tips, and the like—on the same pages as his medical history, whereupon the diaries were presented to the Internal Revenue Service.[3]

The diary for 1968 breaks off, sadly, with Stravinsky's memo of his request for an opera libretto, though he was unable to finish an orchestra piece begun a year-and-a-half before. From November 1968 until the end of his life, the "daily reminders" were written by nurses and only rarely contained more than the records of medications administered.

Except for the details of the expense-accounting, and the blood analyses—the prothrombin time and the figures for hemoglobin, hematocrit, platelet, leucocyte, and red and white corpuscles—the diaries are transcribed complete. On 27 days between January and August 1959, Stravinsky inserted "Entertainment and Promotion Vouchers," and the additional information which they contain is included here. Apart from a few lines in Russian, and very brief excursions into French and German, the language of the original is English. No references are made to composing, and only very exceptionally does Stravinsky mention events of his artistic life. But people are named, and the diaries have some value as a guide to his close friends; thus Christopher Isherwood, mentioned some 36 times as dinner guest or host,

---

[1] 1959. Stravinsky had apparently suffered a third "cardiovascular accident" because of dehydration, the result of a diet against diarrhea ordered by his doctor in Venice.

[2] In London, December 1956, Stravinsky experienced a second thrombosis. His physician, Dr. Symonds, attributed this to smoking, whereupon the composer finally renounced the habit. Dr. Symonds told Mrs. Stravinsky that her husband had no more than a fair chance of living longer than six months—the period, as it happened, during which he composed *Agon*.

[3] Though most of these sums hardly seem worth his time and effort in listing them, it must be admitted that Stravinsky padded even these petty figures. For example, he almost never attended first rehearsals—or, indeed, any except final ones—yet he included taxi fares to all of them as well as to social occasions for which automobiles were provided by his hosts.

appears to be the most prominent figure in Stravinsky's social life. The names that appear most frequently, however, are those of Drs. Sigfrid Knauer (207 visits), Hans Schiff (142 visits), and Max Edel (84 visits, of which more than a third were social). As a rule, Stravinsky mentions his wife only when he is alone with her, or when she is absent, or in connection with her illnesses and doctors' visits. In the 3,375 days covered by the books, Igor and Vera were *not* together on only 29 days.[4] Similarly, Stravinsky usually enters my name in connection with illnesses, absences, concerts, and rehearsals, and, occasionally, on guest-lists at dinner parties. Yet I was with him on approximately 3,200 days.[5]

Some account of Stravinsky's general health in the autumn of 1956, as well as the earliest accounts of the effect of his thrombosis, is a necessary introduction to the diaries. The three reports that follow, from German, Italian, and British doctors, are printed in full.

On November 22, 1956, Professor Dr. Diehl, of the Red Cross Hospital and Maternity Home, Munich, sent the following résumé to Stravinsky in Rome. (The original is in German.)

Mr. Stravinsky appears to suffer from *multiloculare encephalomalacie—mollities cerebri* or softening of the brain brought on by *atherobiatös—arteritisch-thrombotisch*, arthritic and local arrest of circulation of the brain, spasms in the cerebral region. Even if only light, these had clear peripheral or partial paralysis on both sides, but were eventually asymmetrical. The condition may have been aggravated by a viral infection (influenza), and an emotional crisis may have contributed to the ill-effects.

A muscular heart insufficiency is noticeable, with signs of decomposition. The beginning of cirrhosis is evident in the liver, this progressive liver disease being characterized by diffuse damaged cells with modular regeneration. Cirrhosis is associated with a circulatory failure in the liver, and is a result of gastritis and/or stomach inflammation with *Dystermentie*. This damage may possibly be due to an earlier illness, which has left certain still-active amoeba. The patient's medical history indicates a regeneration of amoeba many years ago, but we have not had time to establish proof of this.

There is also a *spondylarthrosis deformans*—inflammation of the investral articulation deviation, deformation of the spine, and neuralgia, or nerve pain, particularly in the head and the nervous ischiadicus. The sciatic nerve is influenced by changing weather.

Examinations have revealed:

Skin	Pale, sinuses well circulated, light *cynnose*, light purplish or dark bluish coloration of the skin and mucous membrane due to lack of sufficient oxygen in the blood. There is an eczema-rash in the anal region.
Head	Free moving, skull not over-sensitive to examination. The eyes move freely, the ears are sometimes blocked but good hearing prevails. Tongue moist, grey white dentures, no problem in the nose.
Neck	No *Sturna*, no goiter, no enlargement of the lymphatic glands.
Breast	Symmetrical, good breathing behavior.
Lungs	On both sides, sidularly deep, unsidular respiratory habits, hypersonorous when tapped. A light breathing noise. Normal voice and vocal sound.
Heart	A slight dilation towards the left, a systolic noise at the top tip. The heart action is regular and the pulse strong and regular. The pressure is 222/135.
Spine	A marked tension in the back muscles.
Abdomen	*Liver:* 2–3 finger-measurement-width enlarged, the consistency thereof is enhanced, the surface is somewhat irregular and slightly painful. A mild painfulness is noticeable around the stomach area.
Extremities	No abnormal alterations. The points are completely flexible.

In the first days the left leg was tested for reflex action. Babinski and the ability to spread the legs, the Gordon & Oppenheim reflexes were negative. The left leg lags behind. Some pain at the sciatic nerve ending. Lasègue lightly positive (normal reaction). In the first days a hyper reflex action of the right arm was observed despite the partial paralysis. The speech is very slightly affected. X-rays showed large symmetrical sinuses and jaw hollows. Those of the neck and spinal region show a bone difference and also an inflammation of the invertebral articulation in the small vertebrae of the spine, also heavy arthritis and inflammation of the neck.

The X-rays of the neck, spinal region, and breast show severe inflammation, and calcification in the region of the aorta leading to the stomach, but for a man of this age no destructive process is proven. Flexibility in both hips is normal at this age. Calcium layers were found in the tubal region (stomach).

The midriff sits deeply and is not easily moveable, the left midriff ripangel does not unfold itself. In the left lung is a layer of calcium spread the size of pinheads and pea sized, but normal according to the blood pressure. On the right is an overall lung fibrosis. At both extremities a rounded callous. Heart moderate with very small regular action. Aorta elongated and sclerotic, though not dilated.

Therapy should include injections of vitamins, massages, and mudpacks, salve for the rash.

[4] Knauer wrote to Vera Stravinsky after her husband's death: "He will continue to carry his creative impulses with him and transform them into something else. Those who were close to him will meet him in another life, as long as we keep the inner bond intact." (May 17, 1971.)

[5] The exceptions occurred as follows:
1956: September 21–28: I.S. is in Switzerland and Germany; R.C. is in Turin.
1957: June 21–July 8: The I.S.'s are in Los Angeles; R.C. is in Boston and Santa Fe.   October 17–19: The I.S.'s are in Donaueschingen and Zürich; R.C. is in Rome.
1958: January 1–8: The I.S.'s are in Houston; R.C. is in Los Angeles.   February 26–March 5: The I.S.'s are in Los Angeles; R.C. is in New York.   July 16–20: The I.S.'s are in Los Angeles; R.C. is in Santa Fe.   September 6–15: The I.S.'s are in Venice; R.C. is in Hamburg and Liège.   September 24–October 1: I.S. is in Lugano, Zürich, Basel, and Bern; V.A.S. and R.C. are in Venice.   October 2–7: The I.S.'s are in Venice, Munich, and Frankfurt; R.C. is in Brussels.   October 24–31: The I.S.'s are in Florence; R.C. is in Hamburg and Vienna.
1959: April 30–May 3: The I.S.'s are in Osaka; R.C. is in Tokyo.   May 20–26: the I.S.'s are in Copenhagen; R.C. is in Los Angeles and Ojai.   June 20–28: The I.S.'s are in Los Angeles; R.C. is in Santa Fe.   October 12–19: I.S. and R.C. are in Naples and Bologna; V.A.S. is in Venice.   October 25–29: The I.S.'s are in Paris and London; R.C. is in Hamburg.
1960: July 26–31: The I.S.'s are in Los Angeles; R.C. is in Santa Fe.
1961: January 18–22: The I.S.'s are in Los Angeles; R.C. is in Toronto.
1962: November 24–27: The I.S.'s are in New York; R.C. is in Toronto.
1964: July 16–20: I.S. and R.C. are in Chicago; V.A.S. is in Los Angeles.   July 20–August 15: The I.S.'s are in Los Angeles; R.C. is in Santa Fe.
1966: February 1–6: I.S. and R.C. are in St. Louis; V.A.S. is in Los Angeles.   July 9–18: The I.S.'s are in New York; R.C. is in Santa Fe.   July 25–August 23: The I.S.'s are in Los Angeles; R.C. is in Santa Fe.

Summary: The peripheral paralysis signs receded within a few days, though a tendency toward headaches, slight dizziness, and general fatigue remained. The blood pressure and the lung pressure . . . have almost completely receded. The size of the liver is slightly abnormal, as is its consistency, but lack of time has prevented a diagnosis of the overall influence of the liver function.

The gastritis has also improved, neurological discomfort being felt only from changes in the weather.

The general prognosis is good, but for the future, psychological and physical care must be taken, a salt-free diet imposed, and less nicotine and alcohol consumed.

The heart and general metabolism should be checked. A repeated treatment with a digitalis preparation is recommended as well as the use of medications for lowering the blood pressure.

On November 30, 1956, Dr. Mario Gozzano, of the Clinica Neuropsichiatrica, Rome, gave Stravinsky the following report. (The original is in English.)

On October 3, the day after he held a concert in Berlin, Mr. Igor Stravinsky was stricken by a sudden right hemiparesis, without any loss of consciousness. Difficulty in word articulation is referred to by the patient; it is impossible to state whether perceptive or receptive aphasia was also present in any degree.

In the following weeks the symptomatology improved gradually to the present conditions. It is difficult to establish if troubles of co-ordinated movements of the right hand were of the ataxic or of the paretic type.

Patient said also that after the episode he felt as if "the left half of [his] face was belonging to another man." [Stravinsky has written in the margin of the report: "I did not say so."] The description of this disturbance is not convincing enough to assume it as a sign of disturbance of body scheme.

At a neurological examination on November 28th I could observe no body oscillations when patient stands with the eyes closed. He can stand on toes with no difficulty. Deambulation with short steps (patient probably walked the same way before the accident) and with a slight flexion of limbs of both sides.

Oculocomotion normal. Pupils of average size and equal. Pupillary reactions normal.

Chewing normal. Slight asymmetry due to a little deficit in the area of the right inferior VII nerve. The position and movements of the tongue are normal. Swallowing, phonotion, and articulation normal. Neck muscles normal.

With upper extremities extended and the eyes closed it is possible to observe a spontaneous flexion of the fingers of the right hand. Muscle strength is slightly reduced in the right hand.

In the lower extremities no evident alterations of segmental motion, although a right Barré is present.

Coordinated movements of upper and lower extremities are normal. Tone normal and symmetrical.

Right radial and pronator reflexes slightly hyperactive. Tricipital symmetrical. Elementary postural reflexes are barely noticeable: good capacity to "relax", to release the limbs.

Right radial and pronator reflexes slightly hyperactive. Tricipital symmetrical. Patellar, achilleus, and adductor normal and symmetrical. Plantar reflex bilaterally in flexion. Abdominal left normal, right diminished.

No superficial (tactile, painful) or deep (postural, vibratory) sensory changes. Patient claims that he cannot perform movements with the same speed as before.

A neurological examination repeated the day after Mr. Stravinsky held a concert in Rome was not modified; only blood pressure was increased (Px—165 mm on November 28th; Ux—190 mm on November 30th).

In sum: mild sequelae of a right hemiparesis are present now (insufficiency of lower facial tendency to asthenic flexion of the finger, Barré, radial and pronator reflex hyperactive, abdominal diminished). No neurological signs are present to indicate any involvement of the left side, as this was noticed in Munich.

Present in the external retromalleolar region of the left foot is a hyperemic, tender oedematous area due to lymphangitis.

According to the history of the acute episode, it is possible to assume that a vascular spasm followed by thrombosis in the area of the *arteria cerebri media* was the cause of the hemiunaresis. The episode happened in circumstances which may give importance as determining factors to physical and emotional stress. Mr. Stravinsky says he was very tired after a concert he conducted in Montreux a few days before Berlin. The cerebral accident happened the day after a performance which kept him in a very intense emotional state. Mr. Stravinsky himself mentioned the fact that all concert performances are preceded by acute anxiety and feelings of fear, a deeply felt emotional condition. In the last days, here in Rome, blood pressure was increased the day after the concert.

The two factors, fatigue and emotion, are of great importance in prescriptions.

Two days before the concert, hemogenic tests gave normal results (prothrombin time 16 seconds). Tromexan in small quantities was administered: 1/2 tab. 3 times in 36 hours. The hemogenic test the morning following the concert gave prothrombin time as 24 seconds, a too marked retardation, in my opinion, compared to the tromexan dosage.

Although we can regard Mr. Stravinsky's neurological condition as normal, his fatigue, his emotional state, especially when he leads concerts, the blood pressure variations under emotional stress, suggest caution to prevent new cerebrovascular accidents. October's stroke was a threatening sign, and the patient recovered with a minimum of sequelae. A new accident, possible unless caution is exercised, could have more severe consequences.

I suggest that Mr. Stravinsky avoid any concert activity for at least a month. This is also Dr. Gilbert's opinion, who has known and followed Mr. Stravinsky for some years. It is also necessary for him to stop smoking, to avoid the spastic activity of nicotine on blood vessels.

A quarter of a tablet, or a half-tablet (if under medical control) of tromexan and a vasodilator (ronicol), and, to decrease anxiety, a half-tablet of Equanil (eventually serpasil), have been prescribed.

Mr. Stravinsky should leave in 40 days for the U.S.A. to prepare and conduct a few concerts. This will be possible only if and when he will follow the rules suggested, especially to rest and avoid any emotional factors.

On December 7 and 11, 1956, Dr. Edmund Symonds wrote the following reports:

Three years ago [the patient] had a prostatectomy. After this he appears to have had a quite severe and protracted episode of vertigo. Since the operation his wife thinks he has never had as much physical energy as before, and during the past year lassitude and drowsiness have been more marked. In the past six months headache has been a new symptom. She has also noticed a redness in the face.

On October 3rd there was a sudden onset of weakness in the right arm and what he calls numbness of the left limbs and left half of the body. At the same time his speech was disturbed. His recollection is that there was a difficulty in controlling his tongue, interfering with articulation. These symptoms appear to have cleared up rapidly. This morning, however, at 6 A.M. he was wakened by a feeling, which he again describes as numbness, in the right half of the body. But there has been no disturbance of speech.

On examination:

He is mentally alert and speech is normal.

The fundi show venous engorgement, but with no appilloedema, nor any hemorrhages.

The visual fields are full to confrontation.

Cranial nerves: the right corneal reflex is diminished, and there is a slight right lower facial weakness, most evident in smiling, otherwise no abnormality.

In the limbs there is no wasting, or dystonia, but there is a little ataxia in the finger-nose-finger test on the right. All deep reflexes are present and equal. Plantar responses flexor.

There is no loss of sensation to cotton-wool or pin-prick.

Postural sense in the toes is good, and vibration sense normal over the tibiae. Two-point discrimination at 0.5 cm. is relatively impaired over the right finger-tips.

The spleen is not palpable. The liver is slightly enlarged, with a soft, rounded margin.

The carotid pulses are strong and equal. Dorsalis podis and posterior tibiae pulses good and equal. Heart sounds normal. No moist sounds in chest.

The blood count yesterday showed:

> red cells 7.6 million
> white cells 10,000
> hemoglobin 140 per cent
> cell volume 61 per cent.

Opinion.

The history of the attack occurring on October 3rd strongly suggests an ischaemic episode in the territory of the basilar artery. The vertigo of three years ago and this morning's episode of right-sided numbness are also consistent with the diagnosis of the basilar stenosis.

Whether he has a polycythaemia vera or an erythrocytosis from some cause not as yet discovered—e.g. pulmonary arteriosclerosis, or the effect of some drug he has been having—rests uncertain at the moment. But the viscosity of his blood must be a factor contributing to the risk of thrombosis. He should, therefore, have a venesection as soon as this can be arranged with a total removal of 25 to 30 ounces.

He may continue to take Equanil in small doses as and when required for the relief of tension, but should not take this regularly. He may continue with his seconal for sleep.

The polycythaemia should be further investigated when he returns to the U.S.A.

The diagnosis of basilar stenosis is inevitably associated with a grave prognosis. He is at risk of a basilar thrombosis at any time, which might be fatal.

December 11, 1956. Since he was last seen he has had a total of 70 ounces of blood withdrawn by daily venesections. Hb yesterday was 125 per cent, with packed cell volume 50 per cent. He feels better in himself and has had no appreciable headache. He still complains of a numbness or wooden feeling involving the right upper trunk and arm and to a lesser extent the hand, but denies any tingling. Possibly the lower part of his right face has been affected by this.

On examination of the nervous system the abnormal signs are as follows: There is still a slight weakness of the right lower face, the right corneal reflex is now equally brisk with the left.

Again there is no weakness, dystonia or ataxia and all the tendon reflexes are equal with flexor plantar responses.

On this occasion temperature sense was examined. Discrimination between hot and cold is normal, but there is a subjective hyperaesthesia for cold over the right forequarter and adjacent trunk. Two-point discrimination as before is a little defective over the right finger-tips, but less so than at the last examination.

Opinion.

He is slowly improving from the effects of the ischaemic episode which occurred on December 7th. This appears to have been confined to the sensory pathway. Its precise situation is uncertain. There may have been a minute area of infarction. But I think it probable that the sensory disturbance will gradually clear up.

His color has improved and the retinal veins are no longer engorged. His own feeling of increased well-being is satisfactory.

Diaries

1956

May

7 [Draft of a telegram.] Tango [*Histoire du soldat*] has no ending: it leads directly to the Waltz, therefore my permission to stop is irrelevant. **27** My *Noces* at Ojai. The beginning of this afternoon concert (outdoor) was under Bob Craft's direction, my arrangement of Bach's Chorale Var. of "*Vom Himmel hoch*''; premiere. **28** Back to Hollywood. **29** Magda Laszlo leaves for N.Y., Rome. Dinner with Arnold Weissberger at "Luau."

June

8 Baggage. Five pieces sent by Rail Express to N.Y. **16** Depart. Red cap, $6, train dinner, $12. **17** Breakfast $2.75, luncheon $8, dinner $10. **18** Luncheon, $2. **19** Arrival in N.Y. Taxi to Gladstone (Hotel). Luncheon (*chez* Maria). Dr. Pierre. Ernest Gold.[6] Dinner (*chez* Maria). **20** Luncheon here (Gladstone). Dinner with Columbia [Records] people (at Maria's). **26** Transportation of the baggage to the pier. **27** Hotel Gladstone bill before leaving to Europe: $394.87.

July

4 Lisbon. Auto promenade. I paid $21, Morton $6.50, Bob $1. Queluz. Lemonade, sandwiches, wine, etc. I paid 82 escures. **9** Tips on boat, restaurant, for the whole trip, $40. **10** Tips to steward and stewardess, baggage, $44. Patras. Spyrakis (agent, driver, secretary, etc.) Restaurant [near] the sea, $6. **11** Cecil Hotel, Patras: $8. To Delphi. A coffee shop and drink at noon: $2. **30** I owe Lawrence $140. Bob owes me $200.15.

August

31 Here, at Bauer Grünwald, with [Luigi] Nono. Dinner with Piovesan.

September

15 Dr. D. at Zürich, Dolder Hotel. **16** Dr. D. *part pour Berne*. **17** Dr. Disraeli [?]. **18** Dr. D. **19** Dr. Dis. Departure for Montreux at noon with Theodore, Denise, Luc [Gilbert]. *Pourboires* Hotel Bauer, Venice, L. 32,500.[7] Lunch at Vicenza. Arrive at Hotel Regina at Stresa. Dinner with Theodore. **21** *Quitte* Hot. Reg.: $22.60. *À* Montreux. **22** *Promenade à Berne* with the Theodores. **23** Return to Berne with Dr.

---

[6] Composer of film music, and husband of the soprano Marni Nixon. Mr. Gold, a fellow patient of Dr. Pierre, knew Stravinsky from Hollywood.

[7] Stravinsky has taped a note on this page signed "R. Craft." "I owe Mr. S. 56,300 lire Sept. 20, 1956." Stravinsky's tabulations are found in Russian beneath this I.O.U.

[Maurice] Gilbert. *Le soir ici (Montreux) à l'hôtel. Diner avec Gilbert que j'ai invité.* **24** First rehearsal after lunch with E. Winkler.[8] Second rehearsal. Supper with Winkler. **26** *Nach* Berlin by plane from Geneva with E. Winkler. N. Nabokov. Hotel am Steinplatz, Berlin. **27** Invited George Balanchine for lunch to speak about my ballet *Agon*.

October

4 To München. Depart 1 p.m. by airplane. Arr. 3 p.m. Tips at departure from Kempinski. . . . Tips arriving Munich. Musica Viva: K.A. Hartmann, Dr. Goetz. Rudolf Albert. Dr. Diehl, 1st visit. **5** Dr. Diehl, 2nd visit, 3rd visit. **6** Dr. Diehl, 4th visit. Dr. Diehl, 5th visit. **9** Arrival of Maurice Gilbert, consultation with Diehl. Cancel concerts in Munich, Zürich, and Winterthur. *Réunion* in Munich (at the hospital of Diehl) until the departure for Vienna (probably with Diehl).

November

21 [Tabulations of cash and traveler's checks]. **27** Proff. Gozzano, neurologist, from the clinique. **28** Visit of Dr. Giuseppe Alessandrini, blood-take. **30** Proff. Gozzano, Dr. Giuseppe Alessandrini, hematologist, 2nd visit, blood-take.

December

2 Leave Rome at noon. Hassler Hotel. [The hotel and other expenses are entered in the hand of Vera Stravinsky.] **3** Paris. Ritz. **4** Arriving London. Examination of the blood. Dr. Stoddard and Dr. Pampignole. **7** First blood-take at 5:30, 15 ounces. Visit in the morning from Prof. Sir Charles Simons [*sic*] and Dr. Pampignole. **8** 2nd blood-take, 15 ounces, Dr. Stoddard. **9** 3rd bleeding, 20 ounces, Dr. Stoddard, and visit of Dr. Pampignole. **10** 4th bleeding, Dr. Stoddard. **11** Went to Sir Charles Simons (he recommends the neurologist Buchard in Los Angeles) for consultation with Dr. Pampignole and Stoddard. Marya Freund, Doda Conrad [his address]. All London hotel bills (about 200 pounds) paid by Boosey & Hawkes to my account for reduction in 1957. **14** Leaving London to Southampton to take S.S. *Mauretania*. **21** Lunch with Victoria Ocampo and René Maheu [United Nations] at Waldorf Astoria. Dinner with Goddard Lieberson at Pavillon.

1957

January

2 From B. & H. $670 (balance of yearly $12,000) to Bankers Trust Co., Park and 57th St. **8** From B. & H. ASCAP (foreign rights) check $6,150. **10** Flowers to Zorina $20.60. *Perséphone.* **13** From N.Y. Philharmonic (for my 3 concerts, Jan. 10, 11, & 13) $2,293.90, after withdrawing of Fed. tax and others from $3000. **16** Theater. Afterwards in St. Moritz with Deborah Ishlon (Columbia) who had invited us to the theater. **17** Theater. Afterwards in the Oak Room. Supper with Deborah Ishlon, who had invited us to the theater. **18** Editing *Perséphone* recording morning and afternoon (with David Oppenheim, Bob Craft, and Brigitta). **22** Sent the baggage to the Grand Central. To Dr. Pierre for blood-take

(by the nurse of Dr. Reddish). **23** [Calculations of expenses during 23 days in N.Y.] Leaving N.Y. for Los Ang. at 6:15 p.m. **24** Changing stations in Chicago. Ph. Hart (Chicago Symph.) for luncheon. **26** Arrival at Los Angeles.

February

1 Dr. M. Edel. **4** Big party [at the S.s'] after Monday Evening Concert. The Dahls, the Harrises (George, with her mother), Dr. Edel, Morton Lawrence [*sic*], Laure Lourié. **5** Dr. M. Edel from 12:30 to 2 p.m. Bad news from Victoria Ocampo: death of her cousin, my good friend Kiki, Buenos Aires. At dinner: Christopher Wood. **8** Dr. Edel. **11** Dr. Edel. Blood from the vein, 5,830,000. Size 55½, color 113. **15** Dr. Edel. 1st vit. C injection. Vit. B12. Vera drove. **16** Dr. Edel. 2nd vit. C inject., B complex. Milene drove. **18** Dr. Edel. 3rd vit. C inj., vit. B12. Monday Evening Concert. Schönberg's Serenade and Monteverdi's *Ballo della Ingrate*. After concert, party at home. 2 Harrises, Morton, 2 Fosses, Dr. Edel. **19** Dr. Edel at 12:30. Vit. C inj., B complex. Milene driving. **20** Dr. Edel at 12. **21** Dr. Edel at 12:15. **22** Dr. Edel at 12:15. **23** Dr. Edel at 12:15. Deborah Ishlon arrived for work on my files. **25** Dr. Edel at 12, vit. C, B12. Blood from the left arm vein (the last time was Febr. 11), 5,900,000. Size 57, color 116. **28** Dr. Knauer 4 p.m. (till 6).

March

2 Dr. Knauer 10:30 (till 12). Dr. Edel at 9:30. Blood-take for examination. At 5 p.m., answer: 5,780,000, 12 hemoglobin. Platelets continue normal, 3,800,000. **5** Dr. Knauer 11:30 (Vera, too, at 12). **7** Dr. Knauer 9 a.m. **9** Dr. Knauer at 10:20 a.m. **11** Dr. Knauer at 5 p.m. **13** Dr. Knauer 5:30. **15** Conductor Leinsdorf's visit at 5. (He will conduct the *Rake* in Holland this summer.) **16** Dr. Knauer 10 a.m. 1st night without seconal. **18** Dr. Knauer 11:30. Drops against *Schwarzegedenken*. **20** Dr. Knauer at 6. **22** Dr. Knauer at 4:30. **24** Dr. Knauer. Special visit at his office at 11 a.m. Blood-take. **26** Dr. Knauer at noon. **27** Dr. Knauer at 6 p.m. **28** Dr. Knauer at 6. **30** Dr. Knauer at noon.

April

1 Dr. Knauer at 10, blood-take. **3** Dr. Knauer, 5:30. **4** Dr. Knauer, 10:30 (after a sleepless night). Injection of nerve cells, Mexican. **5** Good sleep (8 hours). **6** Less sleep, only 5 hours. Dr. Knauer, 11 a.m., injection of nerve cells, Mexican. **8** Dr. Knauer, 11:00 a.m. **10** Dr. Knauer, 5 p.m., blood-take. **13** Dr. Knauer, 10:30, novocaine inject., appendix and prostate scans. **16** Dr. Knauer. Vera 10 a.m., I at 5:30 p.m. **23** Dr. Knauer 5:30. **25** Andre at the brokers at 5:45. **29** Dr. Knauer for Vera at 10:30. **30** Dr. Knauer 3:30. Right hand unsuccessful bleeding [i.e., Knauer could not find a vein]. Mexican injection.

May

1 Dr. Knauer at 5:30. Bleeding, 10 ounces. Mexican hepata cell inj. **2** Dr. Knauer, 5:30. Mexican liver injection. **3** Dr. Knauer, 1:30. Mexican hepata cell inj. **4** Dr. Knauer, 11:30 (Mexican liv. inj.). [In the] back: golden needle.[9] **5** Dr.

---

[8] Erich Winkler was Stravinsky's German concert agent, 1951–56.

[9] Dr. Knauer employed acupuncture already at this date, very successfully in my own case later to restore the use of my right elbow, atrophied after an operation. (R.C.)

Knauer at 11. Mex. hep. inj.   6 Dr. Knauer at 12, blood-take, Mex., hepa. inj.   7 Dr. Kn. at 12. Mex. hepa. inj.   8 Kn. at 10:30. Bleeding, 18 ounces. Hepa. inj.   9 Dr. Knauer at 4:30. 10th hepa. inj.   10 Dr. Knauer at 6:30, hepa inj.   11 Dr. Kn. at noon, hepa inj.   12 Dr. Kn. at noon. Hepa.   13 Dr. Kn. at 11:45, hepa. Begin Royal [queen-bee] jelly.   14 Dr. Kn., Vera at 10, I at 10:45.   15 Dr. Kn at 4:30, bleeding (16 ounces). To Alvin Segal[10] and binder.   16 Dr. Kn. at 12:30. Started hepa beta.   17 Dr. Kn. noon. Hepa beta. Recording Gesualdo. 18 Dr. Kn. at noon. Hepa beta.   19 Dr. Kn. 12, hepa beta. 20 Dr. Kn. at 6 p.m. Blood test. Hepa beta.   21 Dr. Kn. at 11:30. Hepa beta. I started Brazilian whole tablets (one a day).   22 Dr. Kn. at noon.   23 Dr. Kn. 4:30 p.m.   26 Dr. Kn. at 5:30. Bleeding, 15 ounces.   28 Dr. Kn. 12 noon.   29 Dr. Kn 5:30. 1st AGIO injection.   30 Michael Barrie,[11] 11 a.m. Dr. Kn., 4:30.   31 Dr. Kn. 4:30.

June

1 Dr. Kn. noon. 5th time AGIO-GEN. (right side).   3 Dr. Kn. 4:30. Blood examination.   4 Dr. Kn. 4:30.   5 Dr. Kn., 5:30. 6 Dr. Kn. 4:30.   7 Dr. Kn., 4:30.   8 Dr. Kn., 12:30, and Bob, analysis of his urine. In the afternoon, Jean-Pierre Marty, Nadia Boulanger pupil. The Liebersons, Goddard and Brigitta, for dinner at home.   9 Michael Barrie for lunch. In the evening arrival of the television people, Mr. Graff and people.   10 Dr. Kn. 12:30. Bob (Dr. Kn.) 8 p.m.   12 Dr. Kn. 5 p.m.   13 NBC from 9 a.m. till noon, from 1 p.m. till 4 p.m. Dislocated a rib. Dr. Kn. I and Bob.   14 No Kn. NBC till noon (clean up). From 2:30 till 7:30, 1st rehearsal Symph-Wind-Inst., AGON, Symph. Ps., Canticum, Bach Variat.   15 Dr. Kn., I at 10:30 a.m., Bob at 8 p.m. Royce Hall rehearsal from 5 to 7:30.   16 Rehearsal from 2:30 to 7:30, whole program. Arrival of Balanchine.   17 Dr. Kn.: at 1 p.m., Bob; at 1:30, I. Arrival of David Oppenheim [Columbia Records]. Concert at 8:30. 18 Recording of AGON from 8 to 1 a.m. Goldwyn Studios (Formosa and Santa Monica).   19 Worked with Balanchine for AGON. He left at 4 p.m. flying at 9 to N.Y. Recording of Canticum from 8 to 11 p.m. (Columbia Studios).   20 Dr. Kn., I at 1:00, at 2 Bob. Blood examination. In the morning, David Adams. Bob's departure for Boston at 8:00 p.m. by train. 21 Dr. Kn. at 4:30 with Vera who felt tired. I feel strong throat ache, kind of shingles (herpes). Dr. Kn. thinks it is a virus after this terrible week of fatigue.   22 Dr. Kn. at 1:00. Better throat. Lumbago almost disappeared.   24 Dr. Kn 4:30.   26 Dr. Kn. 12:30.   27 Dr. Kn. [for] Vera 4:30.   29 Dr. Kn. 10:30.

July

1 Dr. Kn. I and Vera.   3 Dr. Kn., I at 3:15. At 4:30 was E. Krenek to play me his electronic composition on the Holy Ghost. At 7, Goddard Lieberson to go to "Luau."   5 Dr. Kn. at 1:00. Blood test.   6 Dr. Kn. 10:30, last time before leaving. 7 At the station, L.A.   8 At 1:30, arrive Lamy, Santa Fe. Rehearsal Rake afternoon with orch. (thunderstorm). Dinner with Miranda, Christopher [Isherwood], Bob at El Nido. Three singers for the Rake are the same as 4 years ago in Boston: Anne—Miss Willauer, Tom—Mr. Driscoll, Nick Shadow—Rob. Rue. Baba (excellent young Sarfaty voice).   9 Rehearsal orchestra and singers 2 to 5. Dinner en trois (Vera, me and Bob) at the El Nido.   10 Today only singers, no orch.

Rehearsal in the morning (at 10). A dinner party given by Miranda Masacco at El Nido.   13 Dinner at El Nido with Miranda and her boy friend.   17 No Rake because of the rain.   18 Premiere of the Rake. A very good performance, singers, orchestra, and staging, except horrible light which spoiled (stopped) each applause on its beginning.   19 Meeting with Andre Senutovich and the Secretary of the Santa Fe Opera Association, Ben T. Sanders, at 3 p.m. At 5 p.m. to Babin and Vronsky with Morton and Isherwood. Cold beef before the Rake this evening.   20 Dinner for Miranda at El Nido (with Lawrence Morton, Chr. Isherwood, and 3 others) after it. The last performance (ideal perf. this time). Orch. was good.   21 To New York. Super Chief at 1:30. p.m. Dinner in the compartment.   22 Dinner in the compartment.   23 Arrival N.Y., Gladstone. Starling's Physiology Text Book.   24 Lunch with Deborah Ishlon here in Gladstone, Dr. David Protetch, myself, and Bob. Analysis of blood—bad result. Dinner at Maria's with Huxleys (Aldous and Matthew). Bleeding (18 ounces). Discovery: the Santa Fe altitude and my red corpuscles are 7,000,000.   26 Blood analysis.   28 Day with David Protetch, luncheon, cinema, and dinner.   30 Dr. D. Protetch. Bleeding 16 ounces.   31 Blood examination.

August

1 Sail to Plymouth. Liberté at 4:30. Visit at our cabin: Deb. Ishlon, Dr. David Protetch, Alexis Haieff. We learn of the death of Pavel Tchelichev yesterday in Rome.   6 The last day on Liberté, Dr. (dental service) $3.   22 Blood examination. 24 Rail travels, London—Venice. Leaving London for Paris in the evening.   25 Arrival Paris.   29 Leave Paris in the evening for Venice.   30 Arrival at Venice in the morning. Gondola to hotel on arrival.

September

5 Business dinner with Dav. Oppenheim and his wife at our hotel.   6 Business luncheon with A. Panni (and her son Marcello) of Rome Philharmonia.   11 Arrival of N. Nabokov and Rolf Liebermann with his wife.   14 Dinner with Dick Hammond and George Martin at Martini [restaurant]. Luncheon with the representative of Life magazine, Miss Ruth Lyman.   16 Nadia Boulanger 70 years old. Wire c/o Igor Markevitch, Villars s/Ollon, Vaud, Switzerland. Liebermanns went away (left a memorandum of a contract which he will bring me in Zürich Oct. 20th).   18 Telegr. to Dr. Strobel to Baden-Baden.   19 Blood-take at 10 a.m. in San Marco Hospital with Dr. Comirato accompanying me. My blood pressure 175/100! Lunch with Henri Monnet and his wife. Motoscaffo expense to the hospital and back, L. 4,500.   20 Bleeding, 13 ounces. Blood pressure 165/95.   22 Villa Maser. Contessa Lullig Buschetti at Henri Monnet's at Asolo. Visit to Malipiero. He gave me three volumes of his Monteverdi edition, tome XVI and 2 tomes of XV.   23 Blood test. Blood pressure: 155/90. Torcello. Motoscaffo of the Biennale with Piovesan, W. Congdon. Unforgettable evening.   28 We invited for dinner at Martini Dick Hammond with George Martin, and Piovesan. 30 Leaving Venice at 9 a.m., arriving München at 8 p.m., Hotel Vier Jahreszeiten. Venice—München in autocar.

---

[10] Stravinsky's music copyist, proprietor of the Allegro Music Co., on Vine Street, Hollywood.

[11] The constant companion of Gerald Heard.

2 Dinner with the 2 Hartmanns and Professor Diehl. 4 My concert in München. 5 Departure Munich at 12 (noon) in two cars (one ourselves, another baggage) to Baden-Baden. Arrival in B.-B. at about 5 p.m. Brenners-Park Hotel. 6 Was at rehearsal of *AGON* by Rosbaud at 11 a.m. Dinner with the 2 Winklers of Köln and 2 Strobels here in the hotel (Brenners-Park). 9 From Baden-Baden to Paris, train in the night. Expenses = $365 about. 10 Arrival in Paris. Hôtel Berkeley. Rehearsal at the Salle Pleyel. 11 Concert Salle Pleyel. After the concert, at Mme. Tézenas. 17 Leaving Paris, *le soir à 10:10 WL* [*Wagon Lit*] *à Zürich; Gare de l'Est* (*avec Boulez et Suvchinsky*), *Maurice Gilbert, sa fille, et Theodore venus accompagner.* 18 *Arrivée à Zürich.* Count de Salm comes to welcome us. Oculist for Vera. At 5 o'clock leave for Donaueschingen, arriving at the castle at 7 h. 19 Donaueschingen. Concert at 7, *AGON*, great success. Visit from Karlheinz Stockhausen and Pierre Boulez. Leave for Zürich at 10 in the evening, at the Hotel Baur-au-Lac; 20 1) At noon signed contract with Rolf Liebermann; 2) Lunch with Liebermanns and Nabokov in the bar of the Hotel Baur-au-Lac: 3) Airplane for Rome at 3:30. 4) Arrival at Rome at 7:30 *environ,* at Hotel Hassler. 21 Bob's concert. *AGON* premiere in Rome. 1st rehearsal (evening) at the Foro Italico. 22 Two rehearsals. 23 Last rehearsal. Concert at 9 p.m. 25 Leaving Rome to Paris at 1:50 by train. 26 Arriving in Paris at 9 a.m. Hôtel Berkeley. 29 Early in the morning, 8 a.m., leaving Paris for Le Havre. [Arthur] Sachs's chauffeur to St. Lazare station. The *Liberté.*

November

3 Dinner with Odette Golschman. I paid the wine and extras. Consider as business because of the St. Louis projects and commission (by Vladimir Golschman). 4 Arrival in New York at 8 a.m. Columbia [Records] chauffeur. Gladstone Hotel. 5 Munz Surgical Supplies, 2474 Broadway, Trafalgar 46412.[12] 7 Blood examination by Dr. Protetch. 8 Dr. Protetch bled me, 16 ounces. 11 Blood examination at 11 a.m. 12 Leaving N.Y. at 6 p.m. N.Y. Central Station. Evening meal in our compartment. 13 Breakfast at Chicago. Evening meal at the restaurant. 14 In train. 15 We came home at 9 a.m. to L.A. 16 Dr. Knauer, 1st visit. 18 Dr. Knauer. Vera and I. 19 Had a little temperature. In the evening it was over. 20 Dr. Knauer at 11:30 a.m. 22 Dr. Knauer at 11:30. 23 Dr. Kn. 11 to 12. 25 Dr. Knauer: Vera at 10 a.m., myself at 10:30. 27 Dr. Knauer at 10:30, Vera and myself. 30 Dr. Knauer 1) Bob Craft; 2) Myself.

December

2 Dr. Knauer, 1) Vera at 9:45 a.m., 2) myself at 11:30 a.m. 5 Dr. Knauer at 10:30. My blood-take. Vera came for her hand. Blood analysis. 6 Dr. Knauer. 9 Dr. Knauer, myself, Bob. 16 Dr. Knauer, myself at 12. Dizziness. 17 Dr. Knauer. 18 Dr. Knauer, myself at 11. 19 Dr. Kn. Vera. 21 Dr. Knauer. Myself. Bob. 28 Dr. Knauer, Vera and myself. 30 Dr. Kn., Bob. 31 Kn., I at 4 p.m.

[12] Stravinsky was suffering from an ill-fitting truss.

January

1 [Stravinsky was in Houston to conduct a pair of concerts and to attend an exhibition of his wife's paintings.] 6 Baldwin's tuner came in my absence to tune my two pianos, here at Wetherly Drive, and in Bob's room at the Baroness's. 7 My second concert. After the concert, small supper at Shamrock Hilton Hotel. I invited: Paul Horgan, Miranda, Edward James, Vera, myself. Discussing with James possibilities of composing music to one of his poems. 8 Leaving Houston by plane at 5 p.m. Back home at midnight. Andre and Milene came to pick us up. 9 Luncheon with David Oppenheim at Bel Air Hotel, discussing my recording next spring (*Nightingale*). 10 Dr. Knauer. 14 Dr. Knauer. Vera, Bob, and myself. 17 Dr. Knauer at 11:30, myself. Blood-take. Bob. 20 Dr. Knauer, myself. 21 Dr. Knauer, myself, Bob. 24 Dr. Knauer, myself. 27 Dr. Knauer, myself. 28 Dr. Knauer, Vera. 29 Dr. Knauer, myself.

February

3 Dr. Knauer, myself, Bob. 4 Dr. Knauer, Vera. 5 Dr. Knauer, myself 11:30. 6 Dr. Knauer, Vera. 7 Dr. Knauer 12 noon. 10 Dr. Knauer 11:30, B., 3:30. 12 Dr. Knauer 11:00. 13 Dr. Knauer, Vera. 14 Dr. Knauer, myself. 17 Dr. Knauer. Eugene Lourié and Laure for dinner to speak about *Mavra*. 19 Dr. Knauer. 20 Dr. Knauer late in the evening, a special visit because of a diarrhea. 24 Dr. Knauer. 25 Dr. Knauer. Bob. 26 Dr. Knauer. Myself and Vera. 27 L. Morton. OL2-9792. 28 Dr. Knauer: Blood test. Red corpuscles 5,600,000. Hematocrit 55. Merde! Jan. 17 it was 5,300,000. Hmtcr. 50.

March

1 Dr. Knauer started shots with calcium and sulphur (intravenous injection). 3 Dr. Knauer. Myself. 5 Dr. Knauer. Myself. 6 Dr. Knauer. Vera at 5. 10 Dr. Knauer. Myself. Bursitis. Treatment: 1) shots (special) 2) supersonic. Blood take (last time was Feb. 28). Red corpuscles 5,600,000. Hematocrit 53. 11 Dr. Knauer. Treatment of bursitis. 12 Dr. Knauer. Treatment of bursitis. 14 Dr. Knauer. Treatment of bursitis. 17 Dr. Knauer. Bursitis treatment. 19 Dr. Knauer. Bursitis treatment. 21 Dr. Knauer, bursitis treatment, new hernia belt. 24 Dr. Knauer, bursitis injection. 26 Dr. Knauer, bursitis injection (*no* intravenous injection). 28 Dr. Knauer, bursitis injection. Blood pressure 140/80. Vera consulted him for her feet. 29-30 *Schnupfen.* 31 Dr. Knauer, shot against cold, B.

April

2 Dr. Knauer, myself. 4 Dr. Knauer, myself, blood examination. 9 Dr. Knauer at 11:30. Bleeding. 10 At noon we went to San Francisco. Lunch in Santa Barbara. Arrived at Carmel, Torres Inn Motel at 8 p.m. 12 At 12:30 p.m. we left Carmel. At 4 p.m. we arrived at Clift Hotel in San Francisco. 14 50th wedding anniversary [Mr. and Mrs. Robert Woods Bliss, 1793 32nd St., N.W., Washington, D.C.] 16 Rehearsal at 10 a.m. Concert at 8:30 p.m. After the concert a dinner party. 17 At 4 p.m. Mills College. Show of Afro's painting. St.

Francis Hotel at 6 p.m. My second concert at 8:30 p.m.
18 Third concert at 12:15. Departure to Carmel. Night in
Carmel. **19** At noon, departure for Los Angeles. Luncheon at
Paso Robles. Gasoline expenses Los Angeles—San
Francisco—Los Angeles: $22.04. **21** Dr. Knauer, blood-take
for examination. **23** Dr. Knauer, Vera at 8 p.m., I at 11 a.m.
25 Dr. Knauer, myself, first hepata alpha shot—R.C. **26** Dr.
Knauer, second hepata shot. **28** Dr. Knauer, myself, third
hepata alfa shot. A shot by Mrs. Mack.

May

2 Mrs. Mack did the shot of hepata alfa in the absence of Dr.
Knauer. **3** At Ernst Krenek at 6:30 p.m. **5** Mrs. Mack SH and
H Alfa. Quasi-bursitis left shoulder and knee—kidneys bad
function. **11** Hepata alfa, equanil instead of doriden. **12** Dr.
Knauer—hepata alfa shot for kidneys. Quasi-bursitis. Blood
pressure 142/85, weight 123. **14** Dr. Knauer, hepata alfa shot,
quasi-bursitis, kidneys (better), blood pressure 138/82,
weight 123-and-a-half. Today Dr. Knauer says: "In a few days
your dizziness will disappear"—let us hope! **16** Dr.
Knauer. **18** Dr. Knauer. **19** Dr. Knauer. **20** Dr. Knauer.
Hepata alfa calcium shots. **21** Dr. Knauer 7:30 p.m., hepata
alfa. **23** Dr. Knauer. Calcium shot, hepata alfa. After
Monday's intestinal blood, blood analysis. **25** Dr. Knauer in
the evening. **26** Dr. Knauer at noon. **27** Dr. Knauer, Vera's
visit. **28** Dr. Knauer, heart palpitation. New blood analysis.
29 Dr. Knauer. He sent me to the Cedars of Lebanon for a
blood transfusion, which I did the next day.

June

7 Came back home after ten days at Cedars of Lebanon
Hospital. Dr. Hans Schiff. **19** Blood analysis at Dr. Schiff.
25 At Dr. Jaffe's office, Cedars of Lebanon, at 11:45 a.m.
Injection of radio-phosphate in the left arm (intravenous).
30 Blood analysis at Dr. Schiff.

July

1 My X-ray. No more ulcers!!! **2** At Dr. Jaffe's at Cedars of
Lebanon I took in liquid form the radioactive phosphorus this
second time. **3** Vera's X-rays for the gall bladder stone!
4 At "Luau" with the Sol Babitzes. **5** Luncheon at the
Knauers. **7** At Dr. Hans Schiff—Vera for advice after her X-
ray examination, I for blood examination. **9** At Dr. Henry L.
Jaffe. I took the third time the radio phosphate—liquid form.
14 At Dr. Schiff. Blood take: very slight rising of hematocrit
platelets in slight augmentation. Dr. Schiff gave me a new
injection (muscular) of some cells for my numbness. **15** At
Dr. Schiff, second injection for my numbness. **16** At Dr.
Henry L. Jaffe. I took for the fourth time liquid radio phosphate and paid the bill in the name of Dr. Jaffe $250. **18** At
12 noon at Dr. Knauer. Vera at 5:30 at Dr. Knauer. Myself at
4:30 at Dr. Schiff. **20** Leaving Los Angeles at 9 p.m. with
Andre and Milene and Michael Barrie for dinner at the dining
car on the train. **21** Drinks on the train to invite R. Craft who
conducted my *Danses concertantes* in Santa Fe July 20. **20** At
the Chicago station invited Mr. Paul Fromm to drink and to

eat. **23** Arrival at New York. **25** Dinner with Alexis Haieff.
26 Luncheon at the Ambassador with Dr. David Protetch.
Cinema in Rockefeller Center with Dr. Protetch and his
painter friend.[13] **28** Luncheon with Dr. Protetch.
29 Luncheon at Waldorf. Leaving New York, *Cristoforo
Colombo*.

August

6 I with our hostess Principessa Doria Pamphili. **7** Arrive at
Genoa in Hotel Savoy. **8** Portofino. Luncheon. **9** Leaving
Hotel Savoy in Genoa for Venice. Arrived in Venice at the
Hotel. **11** Installation of a piano in my room. **15** Flowers to
Franz Waxman after his wedding. **16** Dinner at Waxman's at
Gritti (cocktails before at our hotel). **19** Lunch with the
Waxmans at Hotel Cipriani. **25** Motoring to Ferrara with L.
Piovesan.[14] **26** Spend the evening with Madame Kandinsky,
chez Florian (also Nathan Milstein). **27** Luncheon at Cipriani
with [Adriana] Panni and husband. Dinner at Martini,
invitation of Dick Hammond of the *Los Angeles Times*.[15]

September

5 Dinner party given by me for Hammond. **8** Dinner party
with the people of Biennale. **11** Nabokov arrived, luncheon
with him here, at Bauer Hotel. Dinner party with him at Antico
Martini. **12** Early (8 p.m.) to bed. I did not feel well.
13 Dinner with E. Berman. **15** Bought a frame for my
photograph—present to Rolf Liebermann for his birthday.
$7.20. **16** Bought flowers for Vera's show today. $6.20.
20 Dinner party at Danieli for Dr. M. Edel and his wife.
22 Supper at La Colombo with Nadia Boulanger, Alexis
Haieff, and Nicolas Nabokov. **23** Paid $16.00 for a seat at San
Rocco for *Threni* for Nadia Boulanger. **24** Leaving Venice in
an auto car with Dr. E. Roth. Arriving in Lugano at 8 p.m.
25 Leaving Lugano in the train. Arriving in Zürich at 1 p.m.,
Hotel Baur-au-Lac. Theodore, Denise came to see me from
Geneva. First concert *Threni*. **26** Going to Basel for second
performance of *Threni*. Rolf Liebermann driving. Supper in
Basel with Rolf Liebermann. **27** Sick with temperature.
Doctor, pharmacy, etc. **28** Second Zürich performance of
Threni. **29** Last (fourth) Swiss *Threni* in Berne, Hotel
Schwarzerhof. Weber's[16] driver. **30** Dr. Helmut Picard.
Leave Zürich in a car of Weber's at 3:30 p.m. Night at Hotel
Splendide, Lugano.

October

1 Leave Lugano in the car of Weber. Lunch at Lago di Garda
with the chauffeur of Weber. Bill $8.00 with tip. Arrival in
Venice 5:30 p.m. **2** Book binding: $12.00; repair of my
metronome: $3.00; pharmacy: $3.00. **3** Indigestion. Visit from
Dr. Pietro Faccin. **4** Dr. Pietro Faccin's visit. **6** Dr. Pietro
Faccin's visit. Blood pressure 145/95. Lunch with Dick and
George at Martini. American Express took five pieces of our
baggage to send to Claridge's in London. Paid for sleeping
car and tickets Zürich—Firenze for October 21. **7** Leaving
Venice. **8** Leave Munich for Frankfurt. Arrival at Frankfurt
where we met Bob (coming from Brussels). **9** Leaving

---

[13] Russell. A few years later, he married Lotte Lenya.

[14] The widow of Alessandro Piovesan.

[15] Richard Hammond occasionally sent music reviews to the Los Angeles newspaper from Europe.

[16] Carl Weber had commissioned Stravinsky to compose a piano concerto (Movements) for Margrit Weber, the industrialist's wife.

Frankfurt for Hamburg (hotel bill separate). Arrived at Hamburg in the late evening. **10** Rehearsals. **13** My broadcast concert at 8 p.m. Seven concerts with Hamburg orchestra. **14** Leaving Hamburg for Baden-Baden. Payments for car according to understanding with Norddeutscher Rundfunk. Brenners-Park [Hotel] in Baden-Baden. **17** Left Baden-Baden, arrived Donaueschingen by car. **19** Arrived in Zürich, Hotel Baur-au-Lac. **20** Dr. Helmut Picard takes my blood. **21** At the station leaving Zürich to Firenze. **22** Arrived at Firenze, Grand Hotel. **23** Two rehearsals. **24** Two rehearsals. **25** Two rehearsals. **26** Two rehearsals. **27** One rehearsal. Concert. **28** Two rehearsals [for] second concert. **29** Two rehearsals. **30** Second concert. **31** Leaving Florence in car to Venice where taking train (Wagon Lit) to Vienna at 5:50 p.m. Lunch in Bologna.

November

1 Arrival at Vienna. At the station: Frau Altmann and Dr. Seefehlner, photographs and autographs at the station. **2** Two rehearsals. **3** Two rehearsals. **4** Performance. *Oedipus.* **5** Two rehearsals. **6** Two rehearsals. Paid $9.00 to American Consul for certificate given to Austrian taxes saying that I pay American taxes in Hollywood. **7** Concert. **8** Leaving Vienna for Paris. **9** Arrival at Paris. Boulez, Suvchinsky, François-Michel at the station, Hôtel Berkeley. **10** Rehearsals at Salle Pleyel and Mme Tézenas. **11** Three rehearsals. **12** Three rehearsals. **13** Three rehearsals. **14** My concert (*Threni*) at Pleyel (unhappiest concert in my life!). **16** Nabokov, [Arthur] Sachs. **19** Vera paid her doctor $36.00. **20** Leaving Hôtel Berkeley. **21** Arrival at Rome, Hotel Hassler. **24** Rehearsal (*Noces*). **25** Rehearsals. **26** Rehearsals. **27** Rehearsals. Concert at Teatro Eliseo. **30** Leaving Rome for Paris and London.

December

1 Arrival at Paris. Dinner with Mme Tézenas. **2** Arrived at London at 9:30 a.m. Dinner at Simpson's (Strand). **3** Rehearsals. **4** Faber and Faber party. **5** Rehearsals. *Observer* luncheon party. **8** Rehearsals. **9** Rehearsals. **10** Rehearsals. **11** Concert. **14** Leaving Claridge's and London at 9 a.m. for New York. **19** Arrival at New York at 1 p.m., Gladstone Hotel. **20** Doctor, analysis. **22** Doctor myself, doctor Vera. **24** At George Balanchine's with Lucia Davidova. **25** Christmas-New York gratifications Gladstone Hotel $15.00. **26** Food for kitchenette $5.75. **27** Two rehearsals. **28** At "Maria's" dinner with Deborah Ishlon. **29** Rehearsal. Dinner at the Oak Room (Plaza Hotel) with Debbie and Claudio Spies. **30** To Dr. Protetch.

1959

January

4 Concert at Town Hall under Bob's wonderful conducting. American premiere *Threni*. Very big success. Was obliged to bow. Endless boring people. Extreme nervousness. **5** First recording *Threni*. **7** Vera's birthday! [Russian calendar]. **8** Photos taken of Vera and myself by Avedon. Visit of A. Schönberg's son-in-law, Felix Greissle. At Arnold

Weissberger's party. **9** Restaurant "Robert," luncheon with Robert Graffs (Mr. and Mrs.) discussing a film project. **10** Dinner at Ambassador Hotel. **11** Leaving New York to Los Angeles at 2:30 p.m., Pennsylvania Station, via New Orleans. **12** Arrival New Orleans, changing train. Dinner in New Orleans. **14** Arrival at Los Angeles at 6 p.m. **22** 8 p.m. dinner party with Miranda, her husband Mr. Ralph Levy, Rich. Hammond, George Martin, R. Craft, ourselves at home. Television men discussing some future projects.[17] **23** At Dr. H. Schiff at 3 p.m. **24** Dinner at "Luau" with the Waxmans, to discuss my conducting in the spring festival. From 9:30 a.m. *Threni* editing, Columbia Records. At 1 p.m. luncheon with Columbia peole at Brown Derby, John McClure, Bill [Brown], and Robert Craft. **27** Luncheon with Columbia Records people at Brown Derby (Vine Street). John McClure, Bill, Bob Craft, myself. Editing the whole day. **28** At Dr. S. Knauer (sacro-iliac). **29** With the Marions at the Kerr film of the Orient. Afterwards a dinner with them at "Tail o' the Cock." **30** Dr. Schiff.

February

1 Luncheon (at home) in honor of Sascha Schneider (representative of the Fromm Foundation which gave money for the performance of my "Octet" at the Monday Evening Concerts). **2** Monday Evening Concert (with my Octet) and a party afterwards. L. Morton, R. Craft, G. Martin, R. Hammond, I. Dahl (his mother, wife, son), Miranda Levy, L. Lourié's husband, G. Harris and wife (Vartikian), S. & M. Schneider, Sol Babitz, myself and my wife. **3** Dr. H. Schiff. Two musicians from Brussels ("Tail o' the Cock"). **4** "Tail o' the Cock," as yesterday, stage director (London). **6** Milene came to help us (curtains for the den) and typewrite a letter. Drinks (at home) and dinner at "Cock-and-Bull" with Lawrence Morton and Robert Craft to discuss the details of the next Ojai Festival, where R. Craft is conducting my *Rite of Spring*. **10** Dr. Schiff. His nurse gave me a shot. **11** Anticold shot at Dr. Schiff's office. Dentist Briskin, Vera and myself. Dinner at "Luau" with my publisher Leslie Boosey, party with my family. **12** At 6 p.m. Michel Saint-Denis. He is going to stage *Oedipus* with Sadler's Wells in London. **14** At 5 p.m., party for Harold Shapero, his wife, Mrs. Lukas Foss, Leo Smit. **16** At 5:50, our neighbor, William L. Chidester to discuss the question of sewage through a part of our property. Dinner with Hans Popper and Monday Evening Concert with the premiere of Ernst Krenek's *Sestina*. Party after the concert with Ernst Krenek, his wife, Sol Babitz, Mae Babitz, Lawrence Morton, myself, my wife, R. Craft, Hans Popper. **17** Dr. Hans Schiff blood-take and first shot for numbness. At 5:30 Andre coming to meet here Bill Montapert (the young lawyer) to discuss the question about the W. L. Chidester sewer through our garden. Bill Montapert took all the documents of our house to make the necessary investigations downtown. **20** At Dr. Schiff's office, second shot for numbness. With the Marions at Normans's [a restaurant on La Cienega] at 8 p.m. **22** Party with Chr. Isherwood, Don Bachardi, Gerald Heard, Michael Barrie, Aldous Huxley and wife, Matthew Huxley, Stephen Spender and wife, and we 3. **23** At the Cedars of Lebanon for blood tests. Natasha Spender for afternoon tea. **24** Dr. Jaffe. Cedars of Lebanon for radioactive phosphorus. Three o'clock to

---

[17] This statement is not true. Mr. Levy was a film director, but no project with Stravinsky was discussed.

dentist Jerome Briskin. Dr. Schiff, who gave me a deep intermuscular shot for numbness. **25** Dentist Briskin at 5 p.m. **26** Nice evening at Michael Barrie's and Gerald Heard's. Intestinal flu. **27** Dr. Schiff. Blood pressure 150/78. Dentist Jerome Briskin.

March

1 At noon, photographer for social security (J. McConnell Corning). **2** Dr. Schiff in the afternoon. Injections: 1) intravenous calcium; 2) for numbness. In the morning to the Japanese Consulate for visas and to the British for Hong Kong visas. Party after Monday Evening Concert to discuss matters concerning TV projects: R. Hammond, Ralph Levy, his wife, L. Morton, R. Craft, George Harris, his wife, Max Edel, his wife, my wife and myself. **4** Dr. Schiff's office for numbness injection. **6** Shot (numbness) (sacro-iliac). Dinner at Christopher Isherwood. **7** Visit of Mr. Jack Amidor with a Jewish scholar, Joseph Gayer. **8** Disagreeable bowels (four times!) Again! **9** Bad bowels again. Dr. Schiff in the afternoon. **10** At Dr. Schiff's office. A shot for numbness together with vitamins for beginning of a cold. **12** Christopher Isherwood, Don Bachardi, Ralph Levy, Miranda, Bob Craft, my wife, myself. **13** The charity Festival Ball, L.A. Music Festival: L. Morton, Dr. Edel, his wife, Andre Marion, his wife, R. Craft, Marni Nixon, Franz Waxman, his wife, my wife, myself.[18] **16** Cedars of Lebanon for blood examinations at 11 a.m. **17** Dr. H. L. Jaffe. Took a cup of radioactive phosphorous in the division of radiation therapy and nuclear medicine (at Cedars of Lebanon Hospital). **20** Dr. Hans Schiff. Cardiogram good, blood pressure rather high, 175/80-to-95. **22** Visited Darius and Mad. Milhaud at Pacific Palisades. **23** Dr. H. Schiff. Vitamin shot. Blood pressure 148/80. Goodbye party before leaving to Japan, and the last Monday Evening Concert (20-year anniversary): Goddard Lieberson, E. Krenek, his wife, L. Morton, S. Babitz, his wife, David Raksin, his friend, Dick Hammond, George Martin, our family. **24** At "Luau" with Goddard Lieberson. **25** Flight to Honolulu at 9:30 a.m. Nine hours. Arrived at Honolulu at 4:30 p.m. Hawaiian time. Princess Kaiulani Hotel. **28** Leaving Honolulu at noon by Pan American. **30** Arrival at Manila. In the morning, visit of Mrs. Bohlen. In the afternoon, drive with William Morris to a lake and luncheon. Dinner at Ambassador's and Mrs. Bohlen's residence. **31** After luncheon, drive with Mrs. Bohlen. At 6:30 p.m. at the Bohlens' cocktail party and dinner.

April

1 Leaving Manila, arriving at Hong Kong, Repulse Bay Hotel. [Stravinsky has pasted-in a Swiss newspaper announcement of the death, April 1, of Rudolf Kassner.] **5** Leaving Hong Kong at 9:30 a.m., arrival at Tokyo at 4:30. Dinner with David Jones [and Kanetaka Kaoru], Pan American public relations manager. **6** Visit to Amida Buddha at Kamakura, one-and-a-half-hour's drive from Tokyo. Luncheon at Kamakura. **7** In the morning, Vera's meeting with Yakichiro Suma. Mr. Suma (former Ambassador to France) is a member of the National Commission for UNESCO, and the director of Chuo University. **8** Kabuki!!! *Formidable*!!! **9** Rainy excursion to Lake Ashi. Luncheon at Hakone, at Fujiyama Hotel. Dinner with Gasparo Del Corso here in the Imperial Hotel [Tokyo] at Prunier. **10** Crown Prince Akahito wedding. Salvos at 10

a.m. T.V. in the hotel, looking at the procession. In the afternoon with Mr. Richie. Antique shop, Japanese engravings. **11** Bob with Mr. Richie in the car of Mrs. Korn, driving to Nikko. Luncheon with the Raymonds, dinner at Frank Korn's. **12** Leaving Tokyo for Kyoto (Hotel Miyako) at 9 a.m. Dr. Rosenberg's visit at 7 p.m. Arrival at Kyoto at 4:30 p.m. **13** At Osaka. Press conference. Make acquaintance in the lobby of Hotel Osaka Grand of Alfred M. Golden of *The Forward*, "the world's largest Jewish daily." Vienna Opera *Figaro*. Dinner at Alaska Restaurant. **14** Luncheon at Kyoto Hotel. Dinner at Kyoto with Nabokov in Japanese restaurant. **18** Lunch with Nabokov in Kyoto Hotel. **19** Hotel Osaka Grand. To Noh play. **20** Osaka, Bunraku (puppets). **21** Luncheon at Michi Muriyama house, in the garden. At 5 back at Kyoto. **22** Bill of Kyoto Hotel 217,942 yen, Bob 35,100 yen. **23** Leaving Kyoto at 9 p.m. for Tokyo at Imperial Hotel, supper with Nabokov. Son of the owner of the Imperial Hotel, Ichiro Inamaru. **24** Lunch with H. Popper. Japanese dinner with Frank Korn. **25** My two rehearsals. Winds and strings conducted by Bob. After the second rehearsal we went to Nicolas Nabokov to listen to the remarkable Japanese flute and koto. Dinner with Nabokov at Prunier. **26** Second two rehearsals. Conducted by Bob. Dinner with several people (business) $18.00. **27** First full rehearsal from 10 a.m. to 1 p.m. **28** Second full rehearsal from 10 a.m. to 1 p.m. To big Frank Korn party at the Club Kanto. **30** Leaving Tokyo for Osaka at 12:30 p.m. Arrival at Osaka at 8 p.m., Hotel Osaka Grand.

May

1 My first concert at 7 p.m. Supper after concert. **2** Leaving Osaka for Tokyo. **3** At 2 p.m. Sunday my first Tokyo concert. At 8 p.m. dinner at "George's" (good steaks and roast beef). **4** Gagaku ensemble, most impressive old court music, three flutes, three oboes, three chaumes, two kotos, two Japanese lutes, two percussion. And the male dancers: pas-de-quatre and solo. Raw fish and sake with Mr. Tagimoto and Heuwell Tircuit. Dinner party with H. Tircuit and Howard C. (cello). **5** Kabuki with Tagimoto and his silent young wife (not a word in English). In the intermission a snack with sake. Dinner H. Popper, back from Kyoto. **7** My last (third) concert. Dinner with the Frank Korns and D. Richie. **8** Lunch with David Jones at Imperial Viking. Leaving Tokyo at 5 p.m. **9** Arrival at Seattle. Dinner at Olympic Hotel. **10** Leaving Seattle for Los Angeles at noon. Arriving at Los Angeles at 4:30 p.m. One motor of the United Airline plane stopped. Fortunately, the usual landing. **17** At the restaurant "Luau": Dr. M. Edel, Robert Craft, George Martin, Rich. Hammond, my wife and myself. **20** At midnight we left with Vera, Los Angeles for Copenhagen. **21** Arrived in Copenhagen. **22** Rehearsal. **23** Rehearsal. **25** Rehearsal. Concert. Presentation to the King and Queen. Octet. Receiving the press. *Firebird*. Reception at City Hall [with Isak Dinesen]. **26** Leaving Copenhagen, flying back to Los Angeles. **27** Arrival at Los Angeles. **31–June 2** Dr. David Protetch, invited to stay in the motel at Sunset Blvd. for 3 days. Party for him with Dr. and Mrs. M. Edel, and a dinner at "Luau."

June

1 Dr. H. Schiff. **2** Dr. H. Schiff, blood examination. **3** First massage at Dr. Schiff's office. **4** Gerald Heard, Michael

---

[18] Stravinsky's deductions for the people on this voucher are not justified since he was an invited guest himself. (R.C.)

Barrie, R. Hammond, G. Martin, L. Morton, Christopher Isherwood, Don Bachardi, Robert Craft, my wife, myself. **5** Second massage at 9:30. **7** Dr. H. Schiff. **8** Third massage at 9:30. **10** Massage. **14** Luncheon party and, after it, my *Nightingale* rehearsal from 4:30 to 6. A dinner at Bel Air Restaurant: Stephen Spender, his wife Natasha, Don Bachardi, Christopher Isherwood, my wife, myself, R. Craft.
15 Massage. My Party after the last L.A. Music Festival: Mr. & Mrs. Max Edel, George Martin, Rich. Hammond, Mr. & Mrs. Cunningham, Mr. L. Morton, Mr. Ingolf Dahl and son, Father McLane and wife, David Adams, my wife and myself, Rob. Craft, Mr. & Mrs. A. Marion. **17** Massage at 10 a.m.
19 Massage at 10 a.m. **21** Party for the violinist, Babitz, and his wife, the painter, at the restaurant "Luau". **23** Massage. Lambeck. **24** Montaperts at 5:30. **25** Massage Lambeck. 9:45 a.m. **26** Leaving Hollywood for Santa Fe at 9 p.m. Dinner with friends L. Morton and Ingolf Dahl and Milene and Andre before the train. **29** Arrive at Lamy at 2:45 p.m. La Fonda Hotel.

July

2 Diarrhea the whole day in my room at the hotel. **3** Second day diarrhea five times. Vera lunched with Miss Alice Howland and Eleanor Brownell here in the hotel. Mme Vronska (mother) phoned. **4** At 9 a.m. Dr. Kenney. **5** Diarrhea continues. **6** Diarrhea continues. Restaurant El Nido with Paul Horgan. At dress rehearsal of *Madame Butterfly*. **7** Dr. Kenney in the morning, intravenous injection of vitamin B. He phoned in the afternoon to Dr. Hans Schiff (Los Angeles). **10** Dr. Kenney and Dr. Klein for the urine. At 5:20 p.m. Dr. Klein came the second time. Dinner at "Bishop's Lodge." Afterwards at the opera (Mozart's) "*Abduction.*" Wonderful performance! **11** Dr. Kenney in the morning. Shot of vitamin B. **12** Dr. Kenney in the morning. Vitamin B shot. Flowers for Miss Alice Howland, president of the Opera Association of Santa Fe. Concert in the Cathedral of Santa Fe at 8:15 p.m. Bach's *Trauer Ode*, Bob conducting with left hand.[19] Myself *Threni*, conducting with much perspiration. After this concert, supper at our Hotel La Fonda. **13** Leaving Santa Fe, 3:30 p.m. Super Chief at Lamy. **14** Arrival at Los Angeles at 9 a.m., Dr. Schiff at 2 p.m. **16** Dr. Schiff at 2 p.m. blood examination. **19** Dinner party at "Luau," to Dr. M. Edel, Mrs. M. Edel, Robert C., Mrs. Stravinsky, myself. **20** I was at Dr. Schiff to have him phone to Dr. Einstein for X-rays on Wednesday at 10. *It was no consultation.* I asked the nurse to verify the last June bill which seemed to me not to have established a new rate.[20] **22** Dr. Einstein, 300 South Beverly Drive. **27** Mrs. Natasha Spender, Mr. Chr. Isherwood, Mr. Don Bachardi, Mr. R. Craft, Mrs. V. Stravinsky and myself. **30** Dr. M. Edel. First 7½ minutes X-ray treatment of my right arm. At Dr. Joseph Linsman's, who was on vacation and replaced Dr. Trueman. **31** Second X-ray treatment.

August

1 Third X-ray treatment. **3** Fourth X-ray treatment and the final one of my arm. Dr. Trueman expects results in about

three weeks. Evening: Lotte Lenya party. Chr. Isherwood, Don Bachardi, my wife, myself, Rob. Craft. **4** George Balanchine for luncheon with us. **7** Goodbye party for Lawrence Morton with us at Beverly Hills Hotel. **11** Dr. Knauer at 2 p.m. **13** Dr. Knauer. **17** Dr. Knauer. **19** Dr. Knauer. At the restaurant "Luau," dinner party: Dr. M. Edel, his wife, my wife, myself, R. Craft. **20** Bob flying to New York in a jet at 4 p.m. We went with Vera to see the Simon Rodia Towers in Watts. **21** Dr. Knauer at noon. **26** Dr. Knauer at 11:30 a.m. At the "Luau" goodbye party: Mr. Andre Marion, his wife, Dr. Edel, his wife, myself, my wife, R. Craft. **27** Leaving Hollywood for New York with a jet at 1:30 p.m., arriving in New York at 10 p.m. New York time. Supper with D. Ishlon at the Ambassador. **28** After luncheon by limousine (gift of Deborah Ishlon) to Princeton Inn. Dinner party with Sessions. After the dinner visited Robert Oppenheimer. Night at the Hotel Princeton Inn. **29** In the morning my presentation by Sessions to the students of the music department. My conversation with them. Luncheon with Sessions, Robert Graff and his wife. Back to New York. Delayed en route by flooded highways. Car sent to Princeton by Columbia Records. Dinner with Ishlon at the "Four Seasons." **30** Dinner with Dr. Protetch.

September

1 Dinner with Dr. D. Protetch and painter Russell at "Forum." **2** Departure for London. **3** Arrival in London, Claridge's Hotel. **6** Luncheon at Stephen Spender with Isherwood and the painter John Claxton. At twelve noon, visit to Dr. Roth (Boosey & Hawkes). **7** Luncheon at Claridge's with Brigitta and Stephen Spender. Afterwards to Stratford to hear and see *Coriolanus* with Laurence Olivier. Unforgettable. Back to London at 1:30 a.m. At Stephen Spender's some eggs, glass of wine. At Claridge's at 2:30 a.m. **9** Voyage to Edinburgh. **13** Left Edinburgh, Hotel Caledonia, arrival in London at Claridge's. **14** Left London for Paris at 9 p.m. night train. **15** Arrival at Paris, Hôtel Berkeley. **16** Left Paris for Venice. **17** Arrival at Venice at noon, Hotel Bauer Grünwald. **20** Social dinner and party: Hammond, Morton, Lucia Davidova, Berman. **23** Dinner with the Webers at Martini with Dr. Professor Winterstein and wife. **24** Luncheon with Mrs. A. Panni. Arrival of the New York Philharmonic people with Leonard Bernstein.[21] Dinner at Martini with Berman, Theodore and Denise. **26** Dinner at Martini. **27** Dinner at Martini. **28** Dinner at Martini. **29** Dinner at Martini. **30** Vera's name day in Torcello. Luncheon with Columbia photographer, Berman, Hammond, Martin. Dinner at Martini.

October

1 Car to Udine with Columbia photographer. Luncheon at Udine. Dinner at Martini, Venice. **2** Dinner at Martini. **3** Dinner at Martini. **4** Dinner at Martini. **5** Dinner at Martini. **6** Dinner at Martini. **7** Dinner at Martini with Congdon. **8** Dinner at Colombo. Congdon invited. **9** Dinner at Martini. **10** Dinner at Martini with the Hammonds. **11** Last dinner at

---

[19] My right elbow had been broken from a fall on June 24, and I was in surgery the same night. I was released from the hospital (St. Vincent's) on June 30. My arm was in a cast. (R.C.)

[20] Stravinsky is objecting to a charge for a consultation, and to the doctor's prices in general.

[21] Mr. Bernstein, Carlos Moseley, and others representing the Philharmonic met with Stravinsky to offer him a commission to compose a work for the opening of Philharmonic Hall. He declined. The orchestra played a concert at the Teatro La Fenice. Shostakovich's Fifth Symphony and Bernstein's *Age of Anxiety* were on the program. Stravinsky left after a few minutes.

Martini with Hammond and George Martin. **12** Left Venice. To Treviso to take the airplane at 11 a.m. Arriving at Rome at 12:30. Going to Naples by car, arrive at [Hotel] Excelsior at 7 p.m. Eating in the room. **13** Trip to Gesualdo. **14** Trip to Paestum. **15** Noon rehearsal at San Carlo. 7 p.m. rehearsal at San Carlo. **16** Noon rehearsal at San Carlo. 6:30 rehearsal at San Carlo. **17** Rehearsal at noon, rehearsal at 7 p.m. **18** Concert at 6:15 p.m. Leaving Naples at twelve midnight. **19** Arrival at Bologna at 7:40 a.m. Two rehearsals. **20** Rehearsal at Teatro Communale. Vera arrived from Venice in a car at 1 p.m. In the afternoon I felt my right arm and leg very tight and I could not walk normally anymore. **21** Rehearsal at 3:30 p.m. **22** Rehearsal at 10:30 a.m. Concert. **23** Leaving Bologna with a car to Milan. Dinner in Milan at Savigni. **24** Arrival at Paris at Berkeley. **26** Left Paris in the evening for London. **27** Very stormy sea. We arrived in London at 7 p.m. instead of 9 a.m. Ritz Hotel.

November

4 Two rehearsals. **5** Two rehearsals. **6** Two rehearsals. **7** In the BBC Studio Symphony in C and *Oedipus Rex* tape recording to be broadcast later. **9** *Oedipus Rex* in Festival Hall 11 p.m. **13** Leaving London at noon for Southampton Station to tender to *Liberté*. **17** Radiogram to Columbia Records (McClure). **19** Arrival at New York at 10 a.m., Hotel Gladstone. **21** Visit to Dr. Shukoff with Dr. Protetch at noon. In the afternoon, massage by Mr. Dahlgren. Dinner at the "Four Seasons" with D. Ishlon. **23** Luncheon with Goddard Lieberson, invitation at "Voisin." Vera felt badly. I went to bring Dr. Protetch. **24** Vera went to Dr. Protetch at 11 a.m. Karl Dahlgren. Luncheon L. Libman invitation. Piano delivery in my room at Gladstone by Baldwin. Evening at *Gypsy* with Lillian Libman (invited by her). Supper at Ambassador. **25** Dinner with Popper and his family at "Four Seasons." **26** At 2:30 p.m. massage. At Lucia Davidova Thanksgiving dinner. **27** Luncheon here in Gladstone with Bill Brown. Went with him to Museum of Modern Art to see the stupid and provincial Russian film *Ivan the Terrible*, first part, a very embarrassing music by Prokofiev. Dinner at the Gladstone with Lillian Libman discussing the Weber problem (recording Movements with Columbia) and sending a cable to Karl Weber in answer to his letter of November 12. **28** 4:30 p.m. massage. **29** We had a luncheon with Dr. David Protetch. **30** Massage 11:45 a.m.

December

1 Massage 10:45 a.m. Luncheon with Lillian Libman, Sardi East. Dinner at the "Brasserie." **3** Massage 10:45 a.m. At the "Three Crowns" (Swedish restaurant) with Alexis Haieff. Supper at the Ambassador after the theater (*Redhead*) with L. Libman. **4** Massage 10:45 a.m. I and Vera. **5** Massage 9:45 a.m. **7** Massage 10:30 a.m. Vera too. Bad day for me, diarrhea. We were visited by D. Ishlon for a dinner at the Ambassador. **8** Massage at 10:30 a.m. Dinner party by Lieberson at "Caravelle." **9** Massage at 10:30 a.m. Dr. Protetch office blood-take. Supper with Lillian Libman after *Ben Hur*. **10** Massage at 10:30 and Vera. Dinner at "Maria" with P[hilippe] Lambert and Al. Haieff. **11** Rehearse *Noces* at 10 a.m. At 5:30 p.m. Dr. Rappaport (sent by Dr. Protetch)

gave me a shot. At 7 p.m. Auden and Kallman and Lincoln Kirstein. Hors d'oeuvres and gin. **12** Massage at 9:45 a.m. Theater: *Five-Finger Exercise* (John Gielgud) with Debbie Ishlon. Afterwards at Ambassador. **13** Between 12 and 1 p.m. Dr. Rappaport for a shot. Dinner at "Maria" with singer Regina Sarfaty. **14** Massage 10:30 a.m. Rehearsal at 2 p.m. Dinner with Lillian Libman. Chinese film, a propaganda bore. **15** Massage 10:45 a.m. Rehearsal here at Gladstone, *Monteverdi*. **16** Massage 11 a.m. Rehearsal in morning at Gladstone of Monteverdi. Rehearsal at Town Hall at 1:30. At six, a party of J. Harrison, the Dushkins, Alexis, etc. **17** Massage 10:45 a.m. 3 o'clock Dr. Protetch. **18** Massage 10:45. **19** Rehearsal at 9 a.m. Dinner at Ambassador with Deborah Ishlon. **20** Massage at 10:30 a.m. First concert *Noces*. Frames for the four composers who played my *Noces*. $82.18. Party afterward. **21** Massage 10:45. **30** Massage at 10:00 a.m. Paid for massages to Karl G. Dahlgren $200.00. **31** Rehearse at 2 p.m. Dinner with D. Ishlon here in the hotel, and New Year's party with her and other friends.

1960

January

2 Carnegie Hall rehearsal (*Sacre*). **3** At 5:30 my concert at Carnegie Hall with *Sacre*. After the concert a dinner party with the Liebersons and Isaiah Berlin and his wife, at "Voisin's." **4** Television program: conducted from *Firebird* "Dance, Lullaby, and Finale."[22] **8** At the Ambassador Hotel with Victoria Ocampo. **9** Rehearsal at Columbia Studio. We were invited by the Webers for a dinner with [their] friend Thea Dispeker at the "Four Seasons." **11** At the "Four Seasons," dinner with Lucia Davidova, Dick Hammond, George Martin, and the three of us. **12** *Visite d'adieu aux Webers au Savoy Plaza*. **16** Dinner with Hans Popper, "Four Seasons." **17** At the new Park Avenue home of Dick Hammond. Afterward at Lucia Davidova. **18** Deposit check for *Firebird* performance for TV, $4,000. Leyden[23] show, Marcelle de Manziarly party, Victoria Ocampo party. **19** At the City Center Ballet with Victoria Ocampo (*Agon*), afterwards at Balanchine's with Vera and Lucia Davidova. **20** Luncheon with Miranda and Paul Horgan. Dinner at A. Weissberger. **21** Leaving New York for Los Angeles at 10 p.m., Penn Station. **22** In Chicago. **24** Arrival in Los Angeles at 8 a.m. **26** Dr. Hans Schiff. **28** Dr. Schiff. **31** Dr. Schiff dropped [in] at home to give me a shot.

February

1 With Vera at the Farmers' Market. Arthur Berger and his wife at dinner. **4** At Dr. Schiff for a shot (with Milene). Diarrhea, killed by Dr. Protetch's medicine. **5** Diarrhea, started and stopped by Dr. Schiff's pink and gray tablets, 3,4, daily. With Knauers and Beata [Bolm] to see the Russian nonsense of *Eugene Onegin* (as a film) at Royce Hall. **8** At Dr. Schiff (with Milene) for a shot. **11** Dr. H. Schiff's shot (nurse—unfortunately *not painless*—[after] two days!!). **12** At 9:30 a.m. came two architects with a blueprint for a new room on the terrace, estimated cost $3,000. For dinner McClure, went with him to record first session (3 hours) of

---

[22] Leonard Bernstein had invited Stravinsky to guest-conduct part of a New York Philharmonic program taped on January 2 and aired later.

[23] Mr. and Mrs. Van Leyden were painters and friends of the Stravinskys in Los Angeles during the war and in Venice after it.

Petrushka with Bob. Came back at 11:45 to have a drink, at home. **14** John McClure invited [us] for luncheon at "Scandia." **15** Second session *Petrushka* recording with Columbia. **16** Dr H. Schiff. Dinner with J. McClure at "Luau," Beverly Hills. **17** Third session of *Petrushka* recording. **19** Dr. H. Schiff. **21** *Avec les (Eugene) Louriés chez* "Luau." **22** After Dr. N. Heifetz, I went to Dr. H. Schiff for the blood-take and first five tablets of sintrom. I reported to Dr. Nathan Heifetz that I responded excellently to *P-32 therapy* [but] I had in October 1959 again a basilar stenosis accident with my right leg. **23** Take two sintrom in the morning. Dr. H. Schiff at 4 p.m. **25** Luncheon at Beverly Wilshire. Dr. H. Schiff blood-take for sintrom. **26** Half sintrom. Dr. H. Schiff (Milene driving me). **27** Half sintrom. **28** Half sintrom. Fred d'Osten[24] for dinner. **29** Dr. H. Schiff blood-take at 2:30 p.m. Alas, high blood pressure (200).

March

1 Diarrhea at 5, 7, and 9 a.m. Dr. H. Schiff injection at 2 p.m. Blood pressure better—170. **3** Dr. H. Schiff at 2 p.m. for blood-take and blood examination (for *P-32* therapy). Blood pressure 170. **4** Dr. H. Schiff at 2:30 for injection. Blood pressure 190. Sol Babitz party at "Luau." **5** Luncheon Lillian Libman. **7** Christopher Isherwood with Don Bachardi at dinner. **8** Dr. H. Schiff. Blood pressure 180. **9** At 10 p.m. at night club to hear Johnny Walsh[25] singing. We were with the Edels. **10** In the morning, East Los Angeles to hear Christopher Isherwood lecture about Kipling. Afterward luncheon at "Lucey's" with [Isherwood and Don]. Party at home: Everett Helm with wife, Ingolf Dahl with wife, Ernst Krenek with wife. **11** Dr. H. Schiff blood-take and injection. Dr. Max Edel and wife for dinner. **12** Luncheon at Aldous Huxley's. **15** Dr. H. Schiff blood-take. At "Luau" with Leslie Boosey. **17** Party at Miranda and R. Levy. At "Luau" with the Edels and Mr. and Mrs. Thomas. **18** Dr. H. Schiff for radio-phosphate treatment. Dinner at Isherwood. **19** Conductor Solti with wife to ask questions about *Sacre* and *Oedipus*: he's performing them next week at the Los Angeles Philharmonic. **20** One sintrom. **22** Dr. H. Schiff. Blood-take for sintrom. Lunch with Virgil Thomson, Miranda Levy, and Don Bachardi. **23** Half a sintrom. **24** Isherwood and Don (he will make sketches of me after the dinner). **25** Dr. H. Schiff blood-take. Dinner at Romanoff's with Goddard and Brigitta Lieberson. **26** At 11 a.m. Weingarten (gramophone). One sintrom. **27** Half a sintrom. **28** A dinner party for the Liebersons with Gerald Heard, Jay (Michael) Barrie, Christopher Isherwood, Don Bachardi. **29** Dr. H. Schiff: injection. At 5 p.m. had a visit of both Montaperts. Gave him our will to be changed.

April

1 Dr. H. Schiff. Blood-take and injection. **3** With the Edels at "Puccini" [restaurant]. **4** Monday Evening Concert. Berger, Krenek, Babitz. At "Puccini" after the concert with Edels and Mr. and Mrs. Thomas. **5** Dr. H. Schiff injection. **6** I was at

Bob's recording (Columbia) of A. Berg's string orchestra three pieces of the *Lyric Suite* from 8 to 11:30 p.m. **7** At Isherwood's. **8** Dr. H. Schiff injection and blood-take at 8 a.m. New room starting—foundation, two workers and [architect] Bernstein. **12** Dr. H. Schiff injection, Howard Warshaw[26] for lunch. **13** The Montaperts at 5 p.m. to read the new will. They have to write to the office of the heirs of Aaron Sapiro[27] to ask them to [return] the old will to be destroyed. **15** At Dr. Schiff's office—injection received from his nurse. **19** Dr. H. Schiff blood-take. **20** Passports—downtown. **21** Diarrhea in the night. **22** Dr. H. Schiff injection. Spoke with him about Bob's hepatitis and he advised me to ask the opinion of Dr. Jacobson in New York when Bob will be there in 10 days. **23** Diarrhea better. **24** Accompanying Bob to Union Station—he is leaving for Toronto. At "Luau" with Edels. **26** Dr. H. Schiff injection and bloodtake for sintrom (normal) and for radio-phosphate treatment—latter normal except for hematocrit unfortunately high. Dr. Schiff will speak about it with Dr. Jaffe on Monday May 2. At "Luau." **30** Diarrhea.

May

2 Miranda, Isherwood, and Don for dinner. **3** Leonard Feist at the Bel-Air Hotel at 5 p.m. M. Edel to make my sculpture.[28] **4** At 11 a.m., Cedars of Lebanon Dr. Jaffe's office for a special (radioactive) blood-take. **6** Lunch with Miranda and Edward James. Dr. H. Schiff injection and cauterization of my nostrils' crevice. **8** Dr. Max Edel coming for sculpting his bust at 5:30 p.m. **9** Beata Bolm and Margery in the afternoon. Father McLane and Mary for dinner. **11** At 10 a.m., Milene brought me to the Cedars of Lebanon Hospital for taking blood (Dr. H. Schiff and assistants of Dr. Jaffe) and injection of radio-phosphate. At 4 p.m. I was at home. Dr. H. Schiff phoned me after the analysis, asking me to take one sintrom. In the evening, the visit of [Luciano] Berio and his wife [Cathy Berberian]. **13** At Dr. Schiff. At Sol Babitz's: birthday (17 years) of his daughter. **14** At Gerald Heard's. **16** At 5 p.m. the Montaperts to discuss investments. **17** Dr. Schiff for injection. With Milene to bookbinder, [and Alvin] Siegal. Max Edel for sculpture. **20** Dr. H. Schiff visit. Dr. Edel sculpting and dining with his wife afterward *here, at home*. **21** After normal bowel movement, diarrhea, which I stopped. **23** Intestines still not same. **24** Dr. H. Schiff. Blood test for coagulation. Gave me a shot as usual and recommended me to the care of Dr. H. Mills. Bookbinder with Milene. Andre was here at 6 p.m. [and] we sent a letter to M. Bois (Boosey & Hawkes, Paris) RE *"Chroniques de ma vie"* re-publishing by Denoël. Intestines still not sure. **27** To Dr. H. Mills for injection. **28** Dr. Sigfrid Knauer (lumbago!) at 10 a.m. **30** Dr. Knauer (lumbago). **31** Rehearsal at Schoenberg Hall for *Mass* and *Noces* with the [Gregg] Smith Chorus (and piano). R. Craft conducted the rehearsal.

June

1 Dr. Knauer (lumbago). Rehearsal at Schoenberg Hall. *Mass* instruments only. **2** To Knauer with Bob. **3** Dr. Mills.

[24] The Baron Osten-Saken had known the Stravinsky family in St. Petersburg and had been a friend of Vera de Bosset's since her youth.

[25] Protégé of the Baroness Catherine d'Erlanger.

[26] Painter, good friend of the Stravinskys.

[27] Stravinsky's lawyer from the early 1940s had died a few months before.

[28] Edel, an amateur sculptor, worked for many months on a head of Stravinsky.

Analysis of blood for sintrom by D. Kramer (neighbor). In the evening: rehearsal *Noces* with the instruments (Bob conducting). **4** Dr. Knauer. In the evening: rehearsal *Noces* and *Mass* (with the piano), Bob conducting. **5** Rehearsal at 3, *Mass* with instruments. 1) sculpture; 2) "Luau" with Edels; 3) film (at Pantages). **6** Dr. Knauer. Dress rehearsal in Royce Hall. **7** Dr. Mills possible in the morning for the shot by Dorothy. Very successful concert *Mass* and *Les Noces*. Invited Waxmans, the Edels, and Glenn Watkins with John McClure at "Luau." **8** Lunch with McClure (at Beverly Hills Hotel) and Glenn Watkins and Bob (Vera stayed home). **9** Recording of *Mass* and *Monumentum*, a HELL of 6 hours —from 8 to 1:30 a.m. with 1 hour interval for dinner at "Roosevelt" [Hotel]. **11** Dr. Knauer at 11 a.m., shifted to 10 a.m. Colitis. He gave me some shots in the back to de-spasm the colon, and drops. Bob went at 2: Knauer found his liver in less good condition after this last week's excessive work. Christopher Isherwood and Don Bachardi for dinner. **14** Dr. Mills injection and Dr. Knauer blood analysis. **15** At 2 p.m. telephone from Dr. Mills RE Dr. Jaffe's reaction to my blood count. **16** Dr. Knauer at 10 a.m. **17** Dr. Mills injection. Dr. Knauer: Bob at 5:30 p.m. At Christopher Isherwood. **18** Dr. Knauer at 10:30 a.m. **20** Dr. Knauer at noon (Milene driving me). Max Edel—sculpture. **23** New-room party and dinner with Goddard Lieberson. **24** Television session with Lieberson for Columbia. Dr. H. Mills injection. At 5 p.m. Lucien Wulsin (Baldwin). **25** Dr. Knauer at 10 a.m. *50 years ago* was the first performance of *Firebird* at the Paris Opéra! **26** Wonderful Claude Monet show at the County Museum and a chamber concert (Bob Craft conducting) with the beautiful woodwind (No. 10) Serenade of Mozart. My clarinet pieces well-played. Dinner at Phil. Kahgan with the very dull Vincents and Max Edel with Jerry (Mrs. Edel). We saw old films Kahgan made (at Hollywood Bowl) in 1935, myself, Schoenberg, Klemperer. How far away!!!²⁹ **27** At 11:30 Dr. Knauer. Diarrhea. With Christopher Isherwood at "Kabuki" at the Greek Theater: export stuff (after what I saw in Tokyo last year!). **28** Dr. Mills injection. **29** Dr. Knauer at 10:30 a.m. At "Luau": invitation Max Edel. **30** Dr. Max Edel (blood-take for calcium, phosphate, etc.).

July

1 Dr. Mills injection. I take his letter to Dr. Kenney in Santa Fe, and a provision of medications for Santa Fe. Dr. Edel: calcium injection. Dr. Knauer at 10. **3** Dr. Knauer at 10:30. **4** Dr. Knauer at 10:30. At "Luau" with Andre and Milene. **5** Dr. Edel at 9 p.m. Left Los Angeles for Santa Fe. Accompanied [to the train] by Milene and Andre and the Edels. Heavy headache all night. At 3 a.m.: two aspirin. **6** Arrival at Lamy (Santa Fe). Dr. Kenney's visit to decide about the different shots. **8** Dr. Kenney injection at 10 a.m. **9** Unfortunately I took *one* sintrom [i.e., instead of a half]. **10** I conducted at 10 the orchestra rehearsal of *Oedipus*. **12** Conducting *Oedipus* premiere. Went immediately home (driven by Paul Horgan). **13** Dr. Kenney injection at 10 a.m., blood-take. Vera's blood pressure 150/85, my blood pressure 145/85. Dr. Kenney took blood from Bob for liver examination. **14** Second performance of *Oedipus*. **15** Dr. Kenney injection at 10 a.m.

At 3 p.m. dress rehearsal of our concert in [St. Francis] Cathedral. Haydn Symphony Concertant, Mozart *Prague*, my *Symph. of Psalms*. At 7 p.m. with Paul Horgan to a dinner at Alice Howland's. **17** Cathedral Concert. *Symphony of Psalms*, preceded by Mozart's Symphony 38 (Prague) and Haydn's Symphony Concertant conducted by Bob. After concert a big supper at our hotel, two tables, twenty persons, invitation by our good friend Paul Horgan. **18** Drove with Paul Horgan to Bandelier National Monument, very refreshing picnic at a brook. Home at 4 p.m. Dinner with Paul Horgan, Bob, Bill [Brown], and singers! **19** Dr. Kenney 10 a.m. Two rehearsals, orchestra, chorus, soloists of *Rake* in the theater at 2:30 and 8 p.m. **20** I went to Dr. Kenney's office to show him my swollen left arm with a blue [mark]. He gave Bob a shot. At 2:30 *Rake's* rehearsal in the theater but no costumes. Dinner at "El Nido." **23** Vera's show at 4 p.m. [This is in red ink]. Premiere, *Rake's Progress* at 8 p.m. Brilliant performance! **24** Luncheon at "Bishop's Lodge." Business with Hans Busch, John Crosby, Paul Horgan, and Bob Craft concerning *Histoire du soldat* for the next year. **25** Leaving La Fonda, Santa Fe, with the "Super Chief" at 2:30. **26** Arrived in Los Angeles. Many phones with L. Libman about the horrible Mexican Consulate in Los Angeles. Andre and Milene for dinner. **29** Dr. H. Schiff. **30** Good-bye party: [Robert] Cunningham and his wife ("Sis"), Don Bachardi, Christopher Isherwood, Max Edel, his wife, ourselves.

August

1 Los Angeles to Mexico City. **2** First rehearsal. **3** Two rehearsals. At the Bal y Gays. **4** One rehearsal. Concert at Bellas Artes. **5** Rehearsal at 10 a.m. in the Auditorium. Meeting with official people at Bellas Artes at 5 p.m.: Mrs. Amalia Castillo Ledon, Mr. Celestino Gorostiza. Dinner at Villaseñors.³⁰ **6** At 2:30, rehearsal at the Auditorium Nacional. **7** Second concert at Auditorium Nacional at 11:30 a.m. (12,000 people). Lunch with Lillian Libman at her friend Mr. Webb. Home to sleep, to pack. **8** Left Mexico City at 8 a.m. to Bogota (through Costa Rica and Panama). Arrival at Bogota. Maestro Olav Roots.³¹ Hotel Tequendama. **9** Rehearsal at 9 a.m. [Letter] to Andre: [various matters of account]. *"Autrement tout va bien. Ce qui est dur c'est l'altitude. Dans quelques jours espérons ça sera fini—Lima (bord de la mer)."* **10** Rehearsal 9 a.m. **11** Rehearsal at 9 a.m. [Reception 6:30–8:30, U.S. Embassy.] **12** Dress rehearsal. First concert. **13** Second concert. **15** Leaving Bogota at 10:30 to Lima. Arrival at Lima, Hotel Bolivar. **16** Doctor came at 10 a.m. and took my blood. First rehearsal. **17** Second rehearsal. **18** Third rehearsal. Official party. **19** Fourth rehearsal. Concert. **20** To the airfield. Arrival at Santiago de Chile. **21** Tea outside of the city. Driving with Santa Cruz and Letilie (with wife). **22** Rehearsal. **23** Doctor to take blood. Another doctor to consult; he took at 10 a.m. my blood pressure: 150/80. Rehearsal. **24** Rehearsal. Concert at 7 p.m. **25** Leaving Santiago de Chile in the afternoon (at 4), flying to Buenos Aires. Arrival at B.A., Plaza Hotel. **26** Strong cold. Rehearsal. Dr. Bergolea (at 9 p.m.). He gave me a syrup to take every 6 hours, two spoonfuls, to prevent bronchitis. **27** At 9 a.m. blood-take. Dr. Bergolea's

²⁹ The films of Schoenberg and Stravinsky conducting were made indoors, not in Hollywood Bowl.

³⁰ Eduardo Villaseñor had been a friend of the Stravinskys since the 1940s; his second wife, Laura, since the 1950s.

³¹ Russian-speaking conductor of the Bogota Orchestra.

visit at 8 p.m. Rehearsal.　**28** Rehearsal.　**29** Rehearsal at 10 a.m. Concert at 9:30 with television.　**30** At Victoria Ocampo (San Isidro) from 1 to 6 p.m. At 8 p.m. for a dinner at Jeanette de Erize.　**31** Luncheon [with Jose Luis Borges] at Angelica's [Victoria Ocampo's sister].

September

1 Lunch, invited by [Oscar] Alcazar. Rehearsal. The Mestcherskys[32] and Vera's step-mother at the Mestcherskys.
2 Two rehearsals.　**3** Rehearsal in the morning (at 10). Concert at 5 p.m.　**4** Leaving Buenos Aires at 9 a.m. Arrival at Rio at 4:30, Hotel Ouro Verde, Copacabana.　**5** Dinner I gave to Alcazar.　**7** Leaving Rio at 9:45 a.m. to Brasilia and from there with a jet to New York where we [are due] at 9 p.m. New York time. Through Brasilia, Trinidad, New York (Hotel Gladstone).　**8** Dr. Protetch at 2:30 p.m. Blood pressure 162/76. Dinner with Ishlon at "Four Seasons."　**10** Dinner for Deborah Ishlon [The Sheraton East Hotel].　**11** With Dr. Protetch at a delicatessen before cinema and early to bed.
12 Luncheon with Eugene Lourié (here in Gladstone). Dinner with the Liebersons at "Four Seasons."　**15** At 8:30 a.m., equanil.　**17** Leave Hotel Gladstone at 6 p.m. to fly to Rome. Гlying at 8:30 p.m.　**18** Arrival at Rome in the morning. Taking a car to Venice. At Perugia, staying the night at the Brufani Palace Hotel.　**19** Leaving Perugia, luncheon at Narni. Arrival at Venice (rain! flood!!). Hotel Bauer Grünwald.
20 Dr. Faccin's visit. Business dinner at Martini with L. Morton.　**21** Dott. Giampietro Pesenti del Thei. Luncheon (business with Adriana Panni).　**23** First rehearsal at 11 a.m. Second rehearsal at 9 p.m.　**24** Third rehearsal at 10:30 a.m. Fourth rehearsal at 9 p.m.　**25** Fifth rehearsal at 10:30 a.m.
26 Sixth rehearsal at 6 p.m.　**27** Seventh rehearsal at 11 a.m. Concert at 9:30 p.m. Bob Craft conducting Berg's music, Magda Laszlo singing. I conducting *Monumentum* and *Orpheus*. Tips to the stage people bringing me in a sedan chair up the stairs of Palazzo Ducale.　**29** Diarrhea. Dr. Faccin's visit. Temperature 37.7 at 5 p.m.　**30** Dr. Faccin's visit. Luncheon at Martini for Vera's Name Day: Miranda, Morton, Berman, and ourselves. Temperature 37.6 at 5 p.m.

October

1 Diarrhea.　**2** Diarrhea.　**3** Dr. Faccin's visit at 12:30 p.m. Dr. Roth.　**4** Dr. Faccin.　**5** Dr. Faccin twice. Bad day, temperature, cough.　**6** Blood analysis at 9 a.m. Dr. Faccin.
7 Dr. Pesenti. Dr. Faccin.　**8** Dr. Faccin.　**14** Dr. Faccin. DELUGE [Stravinsky has printed the word in large green letters across two pages, October 14 and 15, and drawn waves around it.]　**16** Small temperature again, 37.2 at 5 p.m.　**17** Dr. Pesenti at 7 p.m.　**18** Dr. Pesenti.　**21** Dr. Pesenti.

November

2 At 8:30 a.m., Dr. Pesenti for usual examination. Too-low prothrombin: 49 seconds or 7%!! [Stravinsky had taken too much anticoagulant.]　**4** Blood examination, prothrombin 17″–76%. Dr. Pesenti ordered me to take today one tablet of sintrom, tomorrow also one tablet, and the next days one half-tablet a day until making a new test November 11.
5 Leaving Venice at 10 a.m. Flood!!! By auto to Genoa. Stop at

Verona for luncheon. Arrival at Colombia-Excelsior Hotel.
6 Nine empty rest days. Visit of Mrs. Lanfranco and her two daughters.　**7** First rehearsal.　**8** At noon, Dott. Zino. Rehearsal.　**9** Rehearsal. Urinalysis.　**10** Dr. Zino. Prothrombin test. Rehearsal.　**11** Rehearsal.　**12** Dr. Zino (third time). At 8 a.m. Dr. Zino phoned me—my urine was all right! First concert at 9:30 p.m.　**13** Send a telegram to Boosey & Hawkes, New York RE A. Copland's 60 years birthday. Second concert at 5 p.m.　**14** Leaving Colombia-Excelsior Hotel, Genoa, at 10:44 a.m. for Rome by train. Arrival at Rome.　**15** Dr. G. Alessandrini at 8 a.m. Prothrombin blood test, 23″–45%. [The page includes Stravinsky's laundry list in Russian.]　**17** Nabokov, Berman, Miranda, and ourselves [for] business dinner.　**21** Rehearsal (Filarmonia).　**22** Rehearsal (Filarmonia).　**23** Dr. Alessandrini at 9 a.m. Rehearsal (Eliseo).　**24** Rehearsal (Eliseo). Concert at Eliseo.　**26** Arrival at Paris, Elysée Park Hotel, 2, rue Jean Mermoz (Rond-Point des Champs-Elysées, *26 au 30 Nov.*, *réservations faites par Jean Rochelle du Berkeley*).　**28** Dr. Thiroloix. 24″–50% prothrombin. Sintrom? Don't remember what I took, one or one-half, after analysis.　**29** Salle Gaveau Concert, Berio's "Differences."　**30** At 7 a.m. [Gare] St. Lazare to Havre (*Rotterdam*). .

December

7 Arrival at New York (Hoboken) with S.S. *Rotterdam*. St. Regis Hotel.　**8** Dr. Protetch (2a East 77). Blood test at 10 a.m. at 39 East 63rd St.　**12** Visit to Dr. Scholl's Foot Comfort Shop.
19 Blood test at Laboratory. First rehearsal (singers in Ansonia Hotel [*Nightingale*]).　**20** Second rehearsal at Steinway Building.　**21** Left New York for Washington in a private car at 12 a.m. Arrived at Washington at 7 p.m., Hotel Jefferson.
22 Two rehearsals.　**23** Two rehearsals.　**24** Rehearsals.
25 Rehearsals. Mayflower at night: eating after rehearsal.
26 Rehearsals. Luncheon with singers. Dinner with Bliss Hebert and his assistant.　**27** Two rehearsals.　**28** From today I had a limousine till end of my staying in Washington. First *Nightingale* performance.　**29** Recording.　**30** Second *Nightingale* performance.　**31** In the morning recording of *Nightingale* from 10 a.m. to 2 p.m. Leaving Hotel Jefferson, arrival at New York.

1961

January

3 Analysis of my blood, David Protetch. Deposit of my Washington honorarium for conducting *Nightingale* twice: $3,000.　**5** John McClure is taking me at 8 p.m. to go to the recording session of my Octet (from 8:30 to 11:30 p.m.). Isaac Stern called today that he will be in Los Angeles (Beverly Hills Hotel) February 21 to stay with me and to record my Violin Concerto.　**7** At 10 p.m. with Milton Babbitt and Debbie Ishlon at the electronic studio of Columbia University. With Ishlon went to Dr. Protetch, feeling not well. Afterwards home lunch with Ishlon—and Vera and to the City Center Ballet (*Monumentum*). Dinner with Dr. Protetch in St. Regis.　**9** Leaving New York (St. Regis) at 9 p.m. Arrival at Los Angeles 2:30 L.A. time!　**10** At Dr. H. Schiff (3 p.m.). Blood analysis

---

[32] The Mestcherskys were friends of Stravinsky from his Biarritz years. M. Mestchersky arranged for Stravinsky's concert in the Casino in August 1932.

and the radio phosphate analysis.   **11** The Montaperts at 5:30 p.m. $30,000 for taxes!!!!!!!   **13** A dinner inviting Dr. Max Edel, his wife, and ourselves.   **14** At dinner: Christopher Isherwood with Don Bachardi.   **15** Milene's birthday, dinner at "Perino's."   **16** Dr. H. Schiff (2:30 with Milene). Dinner at "Luau," invitation by John McClure.   **17** Dinner at home with Michael Barrie, Christopher Wood, Gerald Heard.   **18** Bob flies to Canada [to record Schoenberg's Piano Concerto with Glenn Gould].   **19** John McClure at luncheon. We discussed and organized the recording of *Firebird* for January 23–4–5.   **20** Dr. Mills.   **24** Dr. Mills.   **25** Dr. Knauer, 11 a.m.   **26** Dr. Knauer. Isherwood for dinner. Bob does not feel well (temperature 38).   **27** Dr. Knauer. Bob continued his flu (38), sleeps here.   **28** Dr. Knauer. Bob still sick. Dr. M. Edel came in the evening.   **29** Dr. Knauer.   **30** Dr. Knauer.   **31** Dr. H. Schiff. Vera has temperature—prothrombin blood-take absolutely normal. Dr. gave me a shot and advised me to skip sintrom today. Vera has a temperature 37.5.

February

1 Columbia recording of first and third parts of my Symphony in Three Movements.   **3** Dr. H. Schiff injection with a new computer-determined liquid.   **6** Dr. H. Schiff.   **8** Dr. H. Schiff injection.   **9** Charles Rosen rehearsing my Movements. Afterward he stayed here for a dinner with us.   **10** Dr. H. Schiff injection. In the evening: Recording of *Histoire du soldat*.   **11** Dinner at "Perino's."   **12** Stereo recording (with Charles Rosen) Columbia of my Movements.   **13** E.R.W. Rosenthal, Via Cattori 4, Lugano 33013. Stereo recording of the rest of *Histoire du soldat*.   **17** Dr. H. Schiff.   **20** At Dr. H. Schiff for injection.   **24** Dr. H. Schiff prothrombin blood test.   **26** Vera in hospital. Bob went away to New York, I was at "Luau" with Edels.   **27** Isaac Stern. (Vera's operation; at Milene and Andre's for dinner.)   **28** Dr. H. Schiff with Milene and Andre. *Au restaurant Bellevue*, Santa Monica.

March

2 Vera came back from hospital.   **3** Dr. Schiff.   **7** Dr. Schiff and the eye doctor.   **10** Dr. Schiff and the eye doctor.   **14** Dr. Schiff injection.   **18** Dinner at "Luau" with the Edels and cinema.   **20** Dr. Schiff injection—Dr. Pick (nose) cauterization.   **21** Dr. Schiff injection.   **22** Dr. Schiff injection.   **24** Dr. Schiff injection and prothrombin blood-take.   **25** Dr. Schiff gave me injection at my home.   **26** Dr. Schiff injection (lab) at my home.   **29** Dr. Schiff ordered for today another half of sintrom.   **30** Leaving Los Angeles by jet at 1 p.m. to Mexico. Arrival at Mexico at Bamer Hotel.

April

6 Injection of testosterone.   **10** Leaving Mexico City by jet 9 a.m. Arrival at Los Angeles 12:30 L.A. time.   **11** Dr. Schiff.   **14** At Dr. Schiff. Blood-take. At "Luau" dinner for Mrs. Miranda Levy with the Edels and ourselves.   **17** At 2 p.m. I had a visit of Dr. Giessler from Radio Berlin asking me to agree to be broadcast in September in Berlin (*Oedipus* and *Perséphone*). I agreed and he will write me later to confirm this agreement.   **21** At 2 p.m. at Dr. Mills (Dr. Schiff on vacation) for injection. At 8 p.m. a party: Miranda Levy, Mary Vartikian, George Harris, Max Edel and his wife, R. Craft and

ourselves.   **25** Dr. Schiff at 1:45 p.m. to give urine and one injection.   **28** Dr. Schiff. Blood analysis.

May

3 Cedars of Lebanon. Blood test of radio-phosphate.   **4** Cedars of Lebanon. Blood test of radio-phosphate.   **8** At Dr. Jaffe's.   **9** At Dr. Jaffe's (Cedars of Lebanon) 11 a.m. Received by mouth radio-phosphate. Dr. H. Schiff at 2 p.m. Injection.   **11** Party at home: Michael Barrie, Gerald Heard, Bernard Roberts,[33] Christopher Isherwood, R. Craft, and ourselves.   **12** Dr. Schiff injection.   **16** Dr. Schiff injection.   **18** Aldous Huxley and wife came to the dinner and Gerald Heard and Michael.   **19** Dr. Schiff injection.   **23** Dr. Schiff prothrombin blood analysis good, but bad for radio-phosphate. Dinner party: M. Edel and his wife, Pappaiannou,[34] Peter Yates, Miranda and ourselves.   **24** Dr. Jaffe radio-phosphate.   **26** Dr. H. Schiff injection.   **29** I took half a sintrom by distraction. Dr. Schiff. Dr. for the eyes.

June

5 My concert (Violin Concerto) by Eudice Shapiro. *Symphony of Psalms*.   **9** Dr. Schiff's blood count: bad prothrombin.   **12** Dr. Jaffe's office: radio-phosphate by mouth.   **13** Dr. Schiff: shot.   **16** Dr. Schiff: injection.   **20** Dr. Schiff: injection.   **22** Dr. Schiff: blood test, *good*.   **23** Dr. Schiff.   **27** Dr. H. Mills injection.   **29** Blood test. Prothrombin: to take 1 sintrom daily because the coagulation appears not normal. Radio-phosphate good!!

July

1 Left Los Angeles for Santa Fe (Super Chief at 9 p.m.) Miranda was with us at station.   **2** Arrival at Lamy, Santa Fe, La Fonda Hotel.   **3** Dr. Kenney's visit. 180/85. At 8 p.m. dinner Liebersons, Miranda.   **6** *Oedipus* stage rehearsal without orchestra.   **7** 140/80. Dr. Kenney. Injection, blood test.   **12** Conducting at 8:30 p.m. *Oedipus Rex*.   **14** Dr. Kenney. Blood count: prothrombin good.   **19** I am conducting *Perséphone*.   **20** Dr. Kenney blood test. Prothrombin: too much.   **22** Blood test: prothrombin. By doctor's orders I took one sintrom.   **23** By mistake I took one sintrom.   **24** Dr. Kenney advises me to take half a sintrom.   **26** Dr. Kenney: new prothrombin test good results.   **31** Dinner at "El Nido": Paul Horgan, Brigitta, Frank McGee, John Crosby.

August

2 Dr. Kenney blood-take.   **5** Leaving La Fonda, Santa Fe.   **8** Dr. Schiff injection.   **11** Dr. Schiff injection. Dinner party: Maximilian Edel and his wife, Goddard Lieberson, and ourselves.   **15** Dr. Schiff. Blood test: prothrombin.   **18** At 8:15 a.m. at Dr. Billings for X-rays, till 11:30!! Fortunately everything all right with stomach and small intestines. At 2 p.m. at Dr. Schiff usual injection. At 8 p.m. with the Edels, goodbye dinner party at Hilton Hotel.   **24** Leaving Hollywood for New York by plane at 1:30 p.m. Arrival at New York at 9 p.m. Hotel Pierre.   **25** Columbia Records.   **26** Restaurant with Ishlon.   **28** Luncheon with David Adams and Lillian Libman at the bar of Pierre Hotel.   **29** Blood test [at laboratory]. Prothrombin.   **30** At Boosey and Hawkes.   **31** Luncheon with the Canadian people at the bar of Pierre Hotel. Big dinner:

[33] A Latinist with whom Stravinsky corrected the text of *Oedipus Rex*.

[34] Stravinsky had met him in Athens in 1956.

Ishlon, Babbitt, P. Horgan, Lillian Libman, ourselves, at the Pierre bar.

September

1 Leaving New York at 9 a.m. Car to the pier. S.S. *Kungsholm*. Many visitors. Dr. Protetch prepared champagne for everybody. At 11 a.m. starting to move. **8** Tips to waiters, stewards, etc., ending the trip: $75.00. **9** Arrival at Gothenburg. Flying to Helsinki. **10** Visit to Sibelius home. **11** First rehearsal, second rehearsal. **12** Third rehearsal. Concert. **13** Leaving Helsinki, arrival in Stockholm. Opera. *Rake's Progress*. **14** Prothrombin test: it was OK. Doctor said I have to continue 1, ½, 1, ½, etc. **15** Drottningholm Theatre. **16** Uppsala. Dinner at Svanholm's with Ingmar Bergmans. **17** Visit (luncheon) to Blomdahl's, outside Stockholm. **18** Meeting with the Royal Academy. **19** Two rehearsals. **20** Two rehearsals. **21** Two rehearsals. **22** Two rehearsals. **23** Dress rehearsal. Receiving the order at Swedish Broadcasting Co. for the government. **24** Concert at 8 p.m. **25** Leaving Stockholm for Berlin through Hamburg. **26** Doctor takes my blood for prothrombin examination: 40%!! **27** Rehearsal. **28** Rehearsal. *Perséphone* performance, Theater Am Westen. **29** Doctor: new prothrombin blood test. Second performance. **30** Leaving Berlin to Belgrade.

October

3 Dr. Popovič. Performance of *Oedipus*. **4** Cold!! Temperature 37.8. Dr. Popovič. **5** Second performance of *Oedipus*. **6** Leaving Belgrade, arrival at Zürich, Hotel Eden-au-Lac. **7** Dr. Picard: prothrombin blood-take. Leaving Eden-au-Lac, moving to Baur-au-Lac. **8** Dr. Paul Niehans. **9** With Theodore and Denise at Oscar Reinhart's at Winterthur. Theodore and Denise went away (Geneva). **10** Visits: Victor Reinshagen, Curjel and wife. **11** Sacher and wife. **12** Rehearsal. Suvchinsky. Dr. Roth. Luncheon and Dr. Hurlimann. Dr. Maurice Gilbert. Dinner with Suvchinsky. **13** Rehearsal. **14** Dr. Picard. Blood analysis. Rehearsal. **15** Opera. *Histoire du soldat* performance. **16** Leaving Zürich by plane to London—Savoy Hotel. **19** At 6 p.m. . . . **20** Dr. Stoddard at 9 a.m. At 6:30 he called the result of prothrombin test. Social visit Isaiah Berlins, Oxford. **21** Rehearse at Maida Vale. **22** Rehearse. **23** Visit from Hertog. Rehearsal. **24** 2:30 p.m. rehearsal. **25** Rehearsal 10:30 a.m. Broadcast at 8 p.m.: *Ode*, *Perséphone*. **27** Luncheon with Richard De La Mare (Faber and Faber) and Mitchell. 4:30 p.m.: Dr. Stoddard blood test. Dinner with Cyril Connolly and the Stephen Spenders at the Savoy Grill. **28** Rehearsal. Luncheon, Elizabeth Lutyens and Edward Clark. **29** To concert in Festival Hall. *Perséphone* with Brigitta and Loren Driscoll. Big dinner (Boosey & Hawkes) at Savoy Grill. Finale. **30** Leaving London for Cairo at 2 a.m. **31** Arrival Cairo at 10 a.m. Staying at Hotel Shepheard on the Nile. Pyramids.

November

1 Museum. In the evening with Dr. Seraphim and his friends at a wonderful oriental restaurant. **2** To Alexandria by car. **5** Prince Kukrit. **9** Australia. Arrive at Sidney, Hotel Chevron Hilton. **10** Dr. R.N. Lyons blood analysis for prothrombin. 5 p.m. conference. **11** Auckland. **12** Two rehearsals. **13** Two rehearsals. **14** Dress rehearsal. Concert. **15** Flying to Wellington. 5 o'clock US Embassy reception. **17** Rehearsal of

Octet. **18** Rehearsal. Concert. **19** Leaving Hotel Wellington, arrival at Hotel Chevron Hilton in Sidney. **21** At 11:00 a.m. blood-take prothrombin. **28** Melbourne concert. **29** Leaving Melbourne for Tahiti (by Sydney). **30** Dr. Thooris, Papaeete. Prothrombin test: 49% and Azoteine.

December

4 Dr. Thooris. Prothrombin test 22%. **7** Los Angeles. Dr. Mills housecall at 11 p.m. taking blood. Shot. **8** Dr. Schiff. Blood test. Prothrombin 90%!! Dentist: Dr. Koplin. **12** Dr. Schiff. Blood test for prothrombin. To take one teaspoon milk of magnesia against constipation because of cough remedies. Dentist: Dr. Koplin. **14** Dr. Pick at 1:45 for the ear (left).

1962

January

2 Dr. Schiff. Prothrombin tests 28%. **5** Dr. H. Schiff. Prothrombin: 19 sec.—31%. Hematocrit 42. **6** Concert: Ebell Theater. **7** Leaving (flying) for Toronto through New York (Chicago closed—storm). Toronto arrival at Hotel Park Plaza midnight. **8** Delivery of baggage to Park Plaza Hotel. Reading for the radio fragment of our book with Bob. Evening: some intestinal 'flu. Temperature 37.8. Twice sequinil. **9** No more temperature. 36.4. Rehearsal: *Soldat* fragment with Sascha Schneider. **10** Rehearsals. **11** Rehearsals. **12** Rehearse *Symphony of Psalms*. At 7:00 *Symphony of Psalms* performance. **13** Leaving Toronto. Packing in the morning; driving in a limousine to Buffalo. Luncheon at Buffalo. Flying to Washington at 8 p.m. **15** Prothrombin blood-take, 30 sec.—22%. Luncheon at Mildred Bliss. Drive to Washington, D.C., ceremony. First *Oedipus* rehearsal. **16** State Department reception (party). U.S.A. medal given by Dean Rusk. Rehearsal (*L'Heure espagnol*). **18** Dinner at the White House. Meeting with J.F. Kennedy and his charming wife. **20** Luncheon at Bohlens. Recording from 4 p.m. to 10 p.m. of *Oedipus*. **21** At 5:30 p.m. second performance of *Oedipus*. **23** Leaving Washington, D.C., Hotel Jefferson. Brunch with Washington Opera people. Arrival in New York, Hotel Pierre. **24** Recording rehearsals. **25** Recording rehearsals. Attorney Richard L. Levy (with Mr. Wittman). **26** One and one half sintrom because prothrombin test was 80%. From p.m., *Renard* recording and *Ragtime*. No zimbalom! This will be added later. Until 11 p.m. **27** Samuel Dushkin for lunch. **28** Luncheon with Kyriena Ziloti. Evening: Dr. Protetch, Lillian, Nika Nabokov, the Elliott Carters. **29** Prothrombin tests. Theater with Debbie Ishlon. Supper with her, Nabokov, and E. Carter. **30** Harold Spivacke.

February

1 Blood-take: 18 sec.—75%. A half sintrom. **3** We left New York, Pierre Hotel, astrojet American Airlines. 9:45 Los Angeles. **6** Dr. Schiff. Prothrombin test—22%. **7** 5:00 p.m.: the Montaperts. Gave them Har. Spivacke papers and two checks (33 and 20 thousand dollars for quick buying and selling of stocks). Evening, letter (from Bob) to Graff with typewritten two last pages (libretto) *Flood*. **9** First injection Dr. Schiff. Prothrombin same as before. He advised to take one sintrom each morning. Bought "Lincoln" (trading Jaguar), paid $3,000. With Edels at "Luau," rain. **10** Rain. Reparation of the roof of my studio.   **11** Rain.   **12** Montaperts: 5:00 p.m. Signatures, power to buy and to sell.   **13** 2:00 p.m.: Dr. Schiff, second injection. Letters: Kitty, Suvchinsky.   **16** 2:00 p.m. Dr. Schiff third injection. Prothrombin test, 22 sec.—24%.   **19** After Bob's Monday Evening Concert party at our home: Spivacke, two Stephen Spenders, Morton, Dr. Edel, two ladies, ourselves, Isherwood and Don.   **23** Dr. Schiff and eye doctor injection and prothrombin blood-take 18 sec—32%. 5:00 p.m. Spivacke and the Montaperts. I handed Spivacke over my manuscripts of *Mass* (full score) and *Oedipus* (vocal score). The Edels for dinner.   **26** David Adams back from England.   **27** 2:00 p.m. Dr. Schiff.

March

2 2:00 p.m. Dr. Schiff injection. Full check-up: all was right.   **6** 2:00 p.m. Dr. Schiff injection and prothrombin: 18 sec.—33%.   **9** 2:00 p.m. Dr. Schiff injection.   **13** 2 p.m. Dr. Schiff injection.   **14** George Balanchine.   **15** Worked out with Balanchine *The Flood*. Chez "Luau."   **16** With Balanchine, *The Flood*. With Vera at the dentist. Dr. Charles Koplin. Dr. Schiff (only injection). George Balanchine left us at 9:30 p.m. to fly tomorrow to New York.   **20** 2:00 p.m. Doctor H. Schiff injection. Prothrombin *same*.   **23** 2:00 p.m. Dr. H. Schiff injection.   **27** From now on every day John McClure and TV people for *The Flood*. 2:00 p.m. Dr. Schiff injection.   **28** TV people.   **29** TV people.   **30** TV people. 2:00 p.m. Dr. Schiff injection—prothrombin take: *same*.   **31** TV people.

April

1 At 5:00 p.m. visit of Gunther Schneider-Schott.   **8** Robert Lehman coming from Paris.   **12** George Balanchine for dinner.   **13** John Crosby and Santa Fe people. Dinner Jerry Lewis.[35]   **15** George Balanchine for luncheon.   **17** Prothrombin blood test: 22%.   **18** Left Los Angeles at 4:00 p.m. for Seattle, Hotel Olympia.   **19** Rehearsal.   **20** Rehearsal.   **21** Rehearsal. Concert.   **22** Leaving Seattle by train (through Vancouver) to Toronto.   **25** Arrival at Toronto. Rehearsal.   **26** Two rehearsals.   **27** Two rehearsals.   **28** Two rehearsals.   **29** Russian Easter. Recording (Columbia), concert.   **30** Leaving Toronto in a limousine to New York. Arriving in New York in the night.[36]

May

1 Vera's show.   **2** Blood test. Balanchine. Lunch with Alcazar.   **3** Lunch with David Adams.   **4** At Brigitta's, with Balanchine [and Rita Gam].   **6** Luncheon with Edels and Debbie Ishlon; at 4 p.m. Vladimir Ussachevsky; at 7, Dushkin and Elliott Carters.   **7** Blood-take.   **8** Left New York, Pierre Hotel, on the S.S. *Flandre*, commandant Yves Boju.   **14** *Débarquement* tips.   **15** *Arrive à Paris*, Hôtel Berkeley. Dinner: François-Michel chez Beatrice Rothschild.   **16** Dinner Nabokov.   **17** Depart from Paris for South Africa. To airfield: baggage overweight $291.00.   **18** Arrival at Johannesburg. Carlton Hotel.   **19** Two rehearsals.   **21** Two rehearsals.   **22** Rehearsal. First concert in Johannesburg.   **23** Two rehearsals.   **24** Two rehearsals.   **25** Blood examination: 51%. Rehearsal. Second Johannesburg concert.   **26** Leaving Carlton Hotel, bill paid by Boosey & Hawkes (Mr. Pope).

Leaving for Pretoria.   **27** Rehearsal and concert at Springs for the black people.   **28** Rehearsal and concert in Pretoria.   **29** $\frac{1}{2}$ sintrom. Leaving for Kruger Park vacation with the Hartmanns and Johan van der Merwe in two cars. We are their guests. The rooms at Union Hotel in Pretoria (with our baggage) still ours.   **30** $\frac{1}{2}$ sintrom. Kruger Park.   **31** $\frac{1}{2}$ sintrom. Kruger Park. Left in the morning. Back Union Hotel Pretoria from Kruger Park.

June

1 Leaving Pretoria Union Hotel. Bill paid by South African Broadcasting Company. Hotel baggage tips and transportation to the airfield for Capetown: $17.   **2** Blood analysis, prothrombin.   **5** Tipping everybody leaving hotel: $16. The hotel bill was about $250. Around noon we left Capetown airfield for Rome (via Johannesburg, Salisbury, Brazzaville).   **6** At 4:30 a.m. we landed in Rome, Leonardo da Vinci airfield. Baggage tips at the airfield and the hotel, $3, $2. We came from the airfield by a limousine sent by the Hassler Hotel: ?$. I took a sintrom at 5 a.m. Promenade with Adriana Panni (she drove) at Rocca di Papa. Eat at Hassler alone.   **7** At 8 a.m. Dr. Alessandrini's blood test. After taking my blood he ordered me to take $\frac{1}{2}$ sintrom and to wait till 2 p.m. to know the result and the dosage of sintrom to continue. At Berman's apartment-gallery. Dinner with E. Berman.   **8** $\frac{1}{2}$ sintrom.   **9** $\frac{1}{2}$ sintrom.   **10** $\frac{1}{2}$ sintrom.   **17** Leaving Rome Hassler Hotel (about $782). All kinds of hotel tips: $28. Taxis and baggage tips at the airfield: $2. Arrival at Hamburg, Hotel 4 Jahreszeiten. Baggage $5, taxis and baggage at hotel $2.50.   **18** Hamburg, 4 Jahreszeiten.   **19** First rehearsal. Taxis (to and back) $3.   **20** Second rehearsal.   **21** Third rehearsal.   **22** Fourth rehearsal.   **23** Dress rehearsal.   **24** First performance 3 Ballets.   **25** Second performance.   **26** Third performance.   **27** Fourth performance.   **28** Fifth and last performance.   **29** Leaving Hamburg for New York by air in the morning. Hotel bill (in American check) and doctors and correspondence $970 [and] $143. Arrival at New York.

July

2 Blood test. Prothrombin 54%.   **4** With Dr. Protetch at a musical comedy.   **9** Blood test. Prothrombin 24 sec.—35%.   **10** At Russian Tea Room.   **11** Rehearsal, limousine.   **12** Rehearsal. Limousine. To Lillian Libman, percentage for Africa: $800. Concert in [Lewisohn] stadium.   **13** Lunch with D. Adams. With Goddard Lieberson, dinner and theater.   **14** Dinner (social invitation) at "Capri," Miss D. Ishlon, D. Protetch, etc.   **16** Blood test prothrombin.   **17** Leaving New York, Hotel Pierre, for Chicago, Hotel Ambassador East, New York Central Station. Paid Dr. Protetch $150.   **18** Arrival at Chicago Ambassador East.   **20** Rehearsal.   **21** Rehearsal. Concert.   **22** Leaving Chicago in the train.   **23** Back home.   **24** Dr. H. Schiff blood analysis prothrombin 22 sec.—30%, blood pressure 165/98.   **26** Concert Hollywood Bowl.   **27** Good-bye dinner with Miranda and the Marions. "Luau." Leaving Hollywood for Santa Fe.   **28** Arrival at Santa Fe.

August

1 First *Mavra, Renard, Nightingale*.   **2** Dr. Kenney. Prothrombin test 25 sec.—20%, blood pressure 145/95.

---

[35] The comedian was the proprietor of a restaurant on Sunset Boulevard. When Stravinsky first went there, Mr. Lewis displayed a collection of photographs that he had made from a hidden position during several of Stravinsky's recording sessions.

[36] The airports in Toronto and Buffalo were closed because of fog.

3 Second *Mavra, Renard, Nightingale*. 10 Dr. Kenney prothrombin test. At 4:00 p.m., Carlos Chavez lecture. Evening *Perséphone, Oedipus* last time. 15 4:00 p.m. Roger Shattuck with Hugo Weisgal and Milton Babbitt. 16 *Les Soulimas*! 18 Dr. Kenney, prothrombin test. 21 *The Flood* by Bob in concert (twice) very successful! 22 Leaving "La Fonda" for Albuquerque airfield by car. Arrive at New York, Hotel Pierre. 23 Blood test, prothrombin. 27 Blood test, prothrombin. 28 Left New York for Tel Aviv. 29 Arrival at Tel Aviv at 8 p.m., Hotel Dan.

September

1 Visit (luncheon) at Meyer Weisgal (Weizman Institute).
2 First concert Haifa. Bob—Symphony in Three Movements. I—*Ode, Firebird* suite. 3 Nazareth! Galilean Sea! Capernaum! Nothing left!!!! Only the landscape. 4 Blood test at 9 p.m. Doctor at 10 a.m. ordered one sintrom daily because I am very high, more than normal, but he consented I take till the next blood test a half sintrom daily. To Jerusalem for the concert. 5 U.S.A. Embassy party.
7 Leaving Israel (Tel Aviv) arrival at Rome. Evening arrival at Venice. 8 At noon luncheon with Adriana. At 8 p.m., dinner *en trois* Harry's Bar. 9 At noon Adriana invited us at Cipriani. 10 Dr. Faccin, prothrombin test 22 sec.—60%.
15 8:00 a.m. Dr. Faccin completed blood test. Prothrombin: 19 sec.—68%. 17 We left Venezia at 5:00 p.m. to the airport with a motoscaffo. Arrival at Paris. 18 Lunch and dinner here at Berkeley with different people, my social obligation.
19 Lunch at Plaza Athénée with Lieberson and Samuel Beckett. Dinner with François-Michel. 20 Dr. Thiroloix prothrombin test 38%. 21 Leaving Paris for Moscow.
23 Rehearsal. *Boris* Mussorgsky-Rimsky. 24 Rehearsal. Evening: *Mascarade* by Lermontov. 25 Rehearsal. Visit Ekaterina Furtseva, Minister of Culture U.S.S.R. 26 Rehearsal. Gifts to Moscow musicians. First Moscow concert. 28 Second concert. Entertainment (big party).

October

1 Two rehearsals. 2 Two rehearsals. 3 Dress rehearsal. First concert (second program). 4 Second concert—second program. 5 Leaving Moscow Hotel National for Leningrad. Arriving at Hotel L'Europe. 6 First rehearsal, 4:00 p.m. Second rehearsal. 7 First rehearsal 4:00 p.m. Second rehearsal. 8 Dress rehearsal. First concert. 9 Gifts to Leningrad musicians. Second concert. Leaving Leningrad by train. 10 Arriving at Moscow. 5:00 p.m.: good-bye party.
11 At 2:00 p.m. Khrushchev. Leaving Moscow, arriving Paris, Hotel Windsor-Reynolds. 12 Prothrombin test: 62%. Dr. Thiroloix. Cardiogram normal. Vera's cough: only trachea. Gave her suppositories. Arrival of Rufina Ampenova.
14 Elizabeth Lutyens (wife of E. Clark)[37] and her son for lunch. 15 10:00 a.m., Rufina left for Vienna. Adriana Panni came from Berlin, goes with us to Rome. Leaving Windsor-Reynolds, Paris for Rome. 16 Two rehearsals.
17 Rehearsals. Concert. 19 Dr. Alessandrini. Prothrombin 24 sec.—41%. Lunch at American Embassy (Ambassador Mr. Reinhart). 20 To Perugia, limousine. At 5:00: concert.
21 Luncheon with Bill Congdon in the afternoon. Seeing the pictures of Bill, we bought one. Back in Rome at 5:00 p.m. Dinner at Gigi Fazzi. 22 Luncheon at Panni's with American and Russian Ambassadors. 23 Leaving Rome for New York,

9:00 a.m., arriving New York very late because of headwinds. Hotel Pierre. 24 Noon. Dr. Leon P. Lewithin, M.D., came to Pierre Hotel to see me. 4:00 p.m., diarrhea. 25 9:00 a.m., blood analysis. Prothrombin: 14 sec.—60%. 2:00 p.m. at Dr. Lewithin with Vera: for Vera, to go down with the weight because of her 192 pounds. Her heart excellent. For me: caution with nerves, spasms, and duodenum! In the afternoon a new hernia belt. Toward the evening, diarrhea as yesterday. *Pain* in the intestines, maybe the colon? 26 Noon. Dr. Lewithin came to Pierre Hotel. 28 9:00 a.m. Leave New York for Caracas. 29 Rehearsal. 30 Rehearsal.
31 Rehearsal.

November

1 Rehearsal. Concert. 3 Rehearsal. 4 Second concert.
5 Leaving Caracas for New York. Arrival New York Pierre Hotel. Evening Dr. L. Lewithin. 6 Prothrombin tests.
7 Columbia Records. 8 Columbia Records. 9 Columbia Records. 12 Chorus rehearsal. Evening with Liebersons at "Four Seasons." It was awful! Never come again: New administration. 13 Blood test, prothrombin 14 sec.—64%. Orchestra rehearsal 4:00 p.m. Diarrhea. 14 5:00 p.m. Dr. Lewithin here at Pierre Hotel. Evening rehearsals.
15 Rehearsal. Evening at Russian Tea Room to the party for L. Libman after City Center opera, Gilbert and Sullivan *Gondoliers*. 16 Two rehearsals. Katz approved my belt and will make a new one for change when needed. Isaiah Berlin for luncheon. 17 One rehearsal. 18 *Rake* dress rehearsal in Museum of Modern Art. 19 9:30 a.m., Katz (new belt). Dress rehearsal at Carnegie Hall, *Rake* (four hours!), impossible scenery. 20 Carnegie Hall *Rake* piano rehearsal, chorus singers. Renewed scenery promised by Allen Oxenburg. Blood analysis. Evening *Rake* concert. 21 Columbia.
22 Columbia. 23 Columbia. 27 Blood analysis. Prothrombin, 14 sec.—60%. Letter to Theodore about Rosenthal. Leaving New York for Toronto. Railroad station. 28 Arrival at Toronto. 29 Recording at Massey Hall.

December

1 Recording. 2 9:00 p.m. recording. 3 Recording evening. 4 Left Park Plaza Hotel in Toronto to airfield. Arrival at Chicago airfield. Arrival at Los Angeles. Taxi home. 7 Dr. Mills, analysis of blood. 13 5:30 Columbia people "to take a tape" of my speech to broadcast to Japan. Dinner A.Z. Propes, director of Music Festival of Israel.
21 Dr. Mills, prothrombin test 16 sec.—90%.

1964

January

2 With Arnold Weissberger, dinner and theater. 5 At 5 p.m. leaving New York for Philadelphia in a limousine with Lillian Libman. Arriving in Philadelphia Bellevue-Stratford Hotel. Dinner at 8 p.m. 8 Rehearsal. After the rehearsal, with Lillian Libman in a limousine to New York. With recording people, dine at La Caravelle. Leaving Pierre Hotel in limousine for Bellevue-Stratford Philadelphia with Lillian Libman. 9 Rehearsal at 10 a.m. Concert. 14 Concert in New York. 15 *Milene 50 ans! Nous avons téléphoné à L.A.*

[37] Edward Clark, conductor, friend of the Stravinskys since the 1920s, had recently died.

16 Blood analysis very good! With Vera to Dr. Lewithin.
17 At Dr. Lewithin *Vera*. We eat in our room with L. Libman.
18 At La Caravelle with Stephen Spender.   20 To Washington for the last concert, at 11 by train. Jefferson Hotel.   21 To New York Pierre Hotel. Wheel chair [to train]. Dinner in the hotel with Wystan Auden.   27 Dr. Lewithin, bleeding (he took 250 gr.). Vera's treatment, too. Blood test not good (rising). Luncheon in our room with Sam Dushkin.   28 At 11 a.m., bleeding at Dr. Lewithin.   30 Bleeding at Dr. Lewithin.

February

1 Consultation at Dr. Lewithin with Professor La Rue.
3 Bleeding at Dr. Lewithin.   4 At 9 a.m. full blood analysis. At 11 a.m. at Dr. Lewithin.   5 Packing! Leaving New York for Hollywood. At 5 p.m. in a limousine with Lillian Libman. Wheelchair.   6 Arrival at Chicago. Change of train, to Union Station. Ambassador West for lunch with Chicago people. Evening eating in our compartment.   8 Arrival at 10:15 a.m. at Los Angeles.   10 Blood analysis. Temperature 36.7 at 6 a.m. Temperature 37.2 at noon. Temperature 38.1 at 5 p.m.   11 Temperature at 3:30: 37.6.   12 Temperature at 8 p.m. 36.5.   13 Temperature 35.5 at 8 a.m. Temperature 36.8 at 5 p.m.   17 Blood analysis.   20 A dinner party at home with Christopher Isherwood, Don Bachardi, Bill Brown, ourselves.   21 Dinner at "Chasens," business people.
24 Dr. M. Edel. Blood test.   25 Dinner at home with Laura Huxley and Rose.   26 Dinner at "Chasens." VERIGOR people (two Marions, two Montaperts) and ourselves.

March

2 Blood analysis [Dr. Edel].   3 Montapert. Signed all papers to buy the house of the Baroness [d'Erlanger].   6 Blood test. Dr. M. Edel's brother-in-law in Cleveland, Dr. Deutsch: office, Shaker Heights. At "Chasens" dinner party for Morton— Monday Evening Concerts.   8 Leaving home for Cleveland by airplane at 8:50 a.m. Two wheel-chairs (Vera and myself). At Cleveland, Wade-Park Manor.   10 At 10 a.m., first rehearsal.   11 At 9:30 a.m. second rehearsal. [Afternoon] third rehearsal.   14 Second concert.   15 Leaving Cleveland to Cincinnati by car at 11 a.m. Arriving Cincinnati at 4:30 p.m. at the Hotel Netherland Hilton (where we changed twice the "reserved" rooms).   16 Vera's show.   18 Left Cincinnati Netherland Hilton. Wheel-chairs (Vera and I). Arrived at Los Angeles. Wheel-chairs (Vera and I).   23 Blood test.
26 Dinner party at home for Ernst Krenek, his wife, Lawrence Morton, and ourselves.   29 Dinner at "Chasens" with Marions.   30 Blood test at 8 a.m.

April

6 Blood test. Mr. Benjamin for hernia. My *Elegy for J.F.K.* was performed in the Monday Evening Concerts for the first time by Robinson (tenor) and three clarinets, almost without rehearsals and outside of the program. L. Morton announced its performance (repeated twice) to the public, asking to abstain from applauding. This performance was very gratifying.   11 At 6 p.m., L. Berio and his wife and L. Morton at home till 8 p.m. Drinks, caviar. Afterwards the restaurant "Chasens."   13 I was at Dr. Edel and went with him to Dr. M.H. Rabwin for my hernia.   19 With Milene, Andre at

"Perino's." Dinner Verigor.   20 Blood test. At 2:30 p.m., Dr. Anderson, skin.   21 At 2:30 p.m. the skin Dr., C. Russell Anderson.   22 At 11 a.m., Anderson.   24 At 11 a.m., Dr. Anderson, skin.   26 Big goodbye dinner at "Perino's," Lawrence Morton, Milene and Andre Marion, Max and Jerry Edel and ourselves.   29 Leaving Hollywood for Ann Arbor. Wheel-chair at Detroit, taxi to Ann Arbor. Staying at Inn America [Motel]. First rehearsal *Perséphone*, amateur chorus!   30 Dinner offered to [Glenn] Watkins.

May

1 Lillian Libman arrived. Dinner by Watkins.   2 Diarrhea. First rehearsal *Perséphone* at 10 a.m. At 5 p.m. Soulima's arrival.   3 Russian Easter (XB). Leaving Inn America. 2:30 concert. To Toronto in limousine at 5 p.m. Dinner: Lillian Libman, Glenn Watkins, Bob Craft and ourselves. Arrival at Toronto at 12 midnight, Park Plaza Hotel.   4 To see my film.[38]   5 At 11:30 a.m., Mr. Croombs (Boosey & Hawkes). At 5 p.m., the rehearsal of *Faun and Bergère*. Dinner at the hotel with Lillian Libman and McClure.   6 Lunch cancelled because of a rehearsal of Bob's broadcast of *Mavra* at 1:45 p.m.   7 At 1 p.m. for lunch Croombs. At 6:30 p.m. recording.   8 CBS lunch at the hotel. At 6 p.m. second recording till 12 midnight: *Faun & Bergère*, *Star-Spangled Banner*, *Ave Maria*, *Pater Noster*.   9 Leaving Toronto to New York.
10 Afternoon: Dr. Lewithin visit at Hotel Pierre 8 p.m. With Natasha Nabokov-Shakhovskoy at Russian Tea Room.
11 Blood examination. At Dr. Lewithin with Vera. Doctor took 250 mg of blood. Dinner at La Caravelle with Columbia Records people (Goddard Lieberson).   12 Here at the Hotel Pierre, luncheon with H. Stuart Pope. At 8 p.m. *Hamlet*.
13 Dinner with Claudio Spies in our living room.   15 At 12 noon, with Natasha at Tchelichev show. Lunch with her at Vendôme.   16 Restaurant with business people at Chateaubriand.   17 With Natasha, cinema.   18 Dr. Lewithin, bleeding. Restaurant Sherry Netherlands with Natasha.
19 Blood analysis. Leaving New York for Los Angeles flight at 1:45.   22 At 5 p.m. the Montaperts. At 8 p.m. the new film by Ralph Levy.   23 At 3:30 with Vera visiting new home. At 7 to Christopher Isherwood for dinner.   25 Dinner at home with Sol Babitz and wife, Morton, Berio, ourselves.   29 Verigor business dinner at "Chasens."   31 With Edels, cinema; afterwards "Luau."

June

2 Dinner at Milene. Business dinner with [illegible] and Edels.   8 Blood analysis.   11 At 11 a.m. leaving Hollywood for Denver. Continental flight.   14 Leaving Denver (Brown Palace Hotel). Paid Bob by check of Bankers Trust: $1,247 for professional services of the last months.   15 London lunch at Savoy Grill with Dr. E. Roth and Rufina Ampenova, Rufina taking me to the first recording of *Rake* at 6 p.m. Temperature at midnight: 37.6.   22 Antibiotics at 2:45 a.m., 8:45 a.m., temperature 36.7. Dr. Stoddard for my blood analysis.   27 Rehearsal of *Symphony of Psalms*. Bach Variations? The chorus never rehearsed it. That is the organization of Miss Lalandi's Bach Festivals in Oxford. They did not even know that these Variations were for a chorus.
28 The Oxford concert in car at noon with Rufina Ampenova.

[38] The second documentary made by the Canadian National Film Board in Toronto, Bremen, and Hamburg, in April 1963. The first film was made in Toronto, January 1962.

Bob went with somebody before; he had a rehearsal for *Trauer-Ode* before me. **30** Leaving London, arriving at New York, Pierre Hotel.

July

1 [Stravinsky has pasted a newspaper photograph in the diary, captioned "Pierre Monteux is dead at 89."] **3** Dinner with Goddard Lieberson at Caravelle. **4** Dinner at Hurok [apartment] (Park Avenue). **5** Leaving New York, Pierre Hotel, by limousine. Newark to Los Angeles. Arrival at Los Angeles. **7** Prothrombin test. At 5 p.m. Dr. Edel gave me antibiotics, teramycin. At 7 p.m., second time, at 12 midnight, third time. In the night, temperature with chill, but only 37.6 toward morning and little by little down. **8** Temperature 37 at 9 a.m. I took teramycin with my breakfast. **9** Dr. Edel at 2:30 p.m. Dr. Rubin (I am with Dr. Edel) at 4. At 9 Vera gave me *ookha* (*уха*). I took also four tablets of Milk of Magnesia. **10** Good stool. Temperature below 36. At 4 p.m. Dr. Rubin. He found ear much better. *No alcohol for a few days.* Body feeling lousy! Temperature. **12** Dinner at "Chasens" with Edels. **13** Prothrombin test 15! **17** Prothrombin test: 15. **20** Leaving Chicago (Hotel Ambassador East) arriving Los Angeles by air with John McClure. **21** Prothrombin. **22** Dr. Rubin and X-rays perfectly normal. Dr. Edel came to take blood pressure: 140/80. Dinner at "Chasens", invited Ralph Levy and Miranda. **23** Dr. Edel: bleeding at 11:45 a.m. With Edel at Beverly Wilshire for lunch. Montapert at 5 p.m. The Marions at 6–7. **25** Verigor business dinner at Beverly Wilshire. **27** Dr. Edel blood-take at 11:45 a.m. Dinner at Marions. **29** For dinner Lawrence Morton. **30** Dinner at Jack Quinn with Miranda.

August

3 Blood test. **4** Dr. Edel, bleeding at 12 p.m. **5** Going to bed: temperature 37.7! **6** At noon 36.5: perspiring, perspiring, perspiring. At 5 p.m. [entry incomplete]. **7** Vera felt pain (neuralgic). At Milene with Morton. **8** Vera's neuralgic pain stronger. With the Babitzes to the "Beachcomber." **9** Vera's neuralgic pain even stronger. **10** [Blood test]. Vera went to Dr. Edel. He gave her vitamin B-12 (injection) in big quantity and will continue every day. **14** Morning flight to New York, American Airlines at 11 a.m. with Milene [driving to airport]. At New York limousine [to] Hotel Pierre. **15** Vera spent a good night. Dr. from the hotel at noon gave her a vitamin shot B1, B12, and C. Bob Craft back from Santa Fe. Dinner with Goddard Lieberson, his son, and Edwin Allen, here in our living room. **16** Business luncheon at Sherry Netherlands. **17** At 8:30 limousine leaving Pierre Hotel flying Paris. **21** [Jerusalem]. Dr. Cyril Sherer. 164/84. Vera: 176/85. **22** Dr. 150/72. Vera 184/100. **23** Dr. Sherer at 9 a.m.: 150/82. Vera 175/98. Concert. **24** Dr. Sherer 160/90. Vera 165/105. Leaving Jerusalem at 11 for Cesarea: 45 minutes before arriving we had automobile damage and a taxi came from Cesarea to drive us there. Rest at a wonderful resort city hotel near the sea. At 8:30 p.m. concert. The President of Israel presented me with a golden medal after a speech in Hebrew. I answered in English. **25** Leaving

Cesarea for the airfield at Tel Aviv early in the morning. Leaving Tel Aviv at 9 a.m. El Al to New York, stopping in Athens and London and Halifax (Canada), lack of fuel. Hotel Regency, Park Avenue. **26** Columbia (records) editing. **27** Columbia editing. **28** Columbia editing. Invited for a dinner by Goddard Lieberson at Chambord. **29** Dinner with Lillian Libman after unforgettable film *Becket* (Rich. Burton, and the King of Peter O'Toole). We are revolted by Lillian Libman. **30** Leaving the Regency Hotel at noon, flying to Los Angeles.

September

8 Prothrombin test. Moved to the new home 1218 N. Wetherly Drive, 1st night. **11** *Avec Milene chez Dr. Rubin: on a trouvé mes oreilles en ordre.* **13** Leaving Los Angeles for New York at 11 a.m. **14** Blood-take, Dr. Lewithin 2 p.m. Vera at the Dr. at 4 p.m. Blood pressure *180/110*. He gave her drops and tablets. Dinner with Liebersons at Caravelle. Vera paid. **15.** Leaving NY, Hotel Pierre, for Paris. Arriving Paris at 10 p.m. Limousine from Boosey & Hawkes (Mario Bois). Sunday. **16** Lunch and dinner with various people. *$80.* **17** Leaving Paris for Berlin, Air France. Hotel Kempinsky. **22** Concert: *Renard* (me). *Noces, Abraham and Isaac* (Bob), *Capriccio* with Magaloff (me). **24** Leaving Berlin Hotel Kempinsky, arriving in Paris. **27** Leaving Paris to New York. Limousine. **28** Dr. Lewithin, blood-take 220 gr. **30** Dr. Lewithin blood-take: 215 gr. Vera's Name Day.

October

2 Rain! Limousine, Dr. Lewithin blood-take, 235 gr., at 4 p.m. (with Balanchine).[39] Lunch with Lucia, Natasha, and Mrs. Spies. Lunch at our apartment with Libman. **3** Dinner at Dushkins. Check to Louise for flowers to be presented for a ballet show of mine. **4** At lunch Johnny [Stravinsky]. Afternoon with Natasha and Peter Nabokov to the Lincoln Center Ballet. **5** Leaving NY, Drake Hotel by plane to Los Angeles at 4 p.m. (plane at 6 p.m.). Arrival delayed (front wind) at 9 p.m. L.A. time. Met by Edwin. At home, *new home*, 1218 N. Wetherly Dr. **10** At home dinner with the Edels. **12** Prothrombin analysis: 48%. **13** Dr. Edel at noon. In our car with Otis.[40] **14** Dr. Edel flies to NY for 2 weeks, St. Moritz Hotel. **16** Goodbye dinner with Morton at "Chasens." **17** The Marions went away for a vacation. **19** Prothrombin test. Dr. Edel flies from NY (with instructions for dosage of sintrom). At 6 p.m. the Montaperts. **21** At 11 a.m. Montapert for manuscripts he will bring. **23** Dinner at Ralph Levy (Miranda). **25** At "Chasens" business dinner. **28** At dinner, Gerald Heard and Michael Barrie.

November

5 At 5:30 Montaperts. They took my correspondence with the man from Princeton RE *Requiem*. **6** 4 p.m. Dr. Edel. **7** Mrs. Arn[41] for lunch at home. Mrs. Arn for dinner at the Beverly Wilshire Hotel. **8** Mrs. Arn for lunch at home. Dinner at Lawrence Morton. **9** At 3:30 at Dr. Edel to show him my feruncle. He invited Dr. B. who ordered me to lie down with an electric device on my feruncle and, for the moment, not to

[39] Lewithin was George Balanchine's physician.

[40] A handyman employed by Stravinsky.

[41] Irina Arn procured conducting engagements for Stravinsky in San Francisco, Oakland, Berkeley, Pasadena, and Honolulu. She and her mother spoke Russian with the Stravinskys.

use my hernia belt. Decided to see him again next Friday Nov. 13th at 4 p.m. Marions back after vacation, dinner with us at home. **13** At 4 p.m. at Dr. Edel and the surgeon B. They found the situation better. **20** At Dr. Edel and the surgeon B. **22** Leaving L.A. for NY at 11 a.m., arriving in time at NY, Hotel Pierre. **24** Metropolitan Opera with Lillian (limousine through B. & H.). What a joy! Wonderful performance. **25** Broadway musical comedy with Lillian (limousine through B. & H.). **26** Luncheon for Hurok. French restaurant. **27** Dr. Lewithin. Blood pressure 120/75. Very bad swelling. He found a little stroke (brain!). He couldn't see the arteries in the right eye. **28** Dr. Lewithin. Blood pressure *140/90*. Little better walking. Right eye: he saw the artery a little. Vera's blood pressure *168/112*. Dr. Lewithin at 11:30 a.m. At 10 a.m. prothrombin test and others. 75% very bad!

December

1 Dr. Lewithin at 11:30. Blood-take, 240 gr. **2** Dr. Lewithin at 12 noon, blood-take 240 gr. **4** Dr. Lewithin at 11:45. Blood-take. **6** Our first concert in the new (very bad acoustics) Lincoln Center Philharmonic. Full house, good success, not very good performance. Program: R. Craft [conducting] R. Strauss's *Bourgeois Gentilhomme*, *Abraham and Isaac*; myself, with Cathy Berberian, starting with Isaac Stern, *Pastorale*; canto: *Elegy for J.F.K.*, *Berceuses du chat*, *Pribaoutki*; orch.: *Pulcinella* Suite. **7** To Washington, D.C. by train with Lillian Libman. **8** Leaving Washington, D.C. at 10 a.m. by train, arriving NY at 4 p.m. at Pierre Hotel. **9** By car to Boston with Vera.[42] It took us 5 hours. Hotel Ritz Carlton. Brilliant concert in Symphony Hall, sold out hall. All our old friends there, the Forbes, Arth. Berger, Harold Shapero, the widow of [Irving] Fine, Dr. Rinkel, etc. **10** Left Boston at 10 a.m. for NY, at Pierre Hotel at 3 p.m. **11** Columbia recording (E. 30 St.): 1) Verlaine (*orch. only*—the singer couldn't sing, too high for him); 2) *Pribaoutki* with Cathy Berberian; 3) *Apollo*—pas de deux (remake); 4) 2 trumpets in *Fanfare*. **12** Outside temperature 52, raining. At Liebersons' for dinner. **14** Prothrombin test at 9:30 a.m. 37. Recording with Cathy Berberian: 1) *Berceuses du chat*, 2) *Elegy J.F.K.*, 3) Shakespeare Songs. Dinner at Cathy Berberian restaurant [her parents' restaurant]. **16** Dinner at Pavillon with McClures. **17** David Oppenheim at 4:30. Dinner with Liebersons at La Caravelle. **20** At Dick Hammond's. **21** Prothrombin test: Dr. Lewithin at 12 noon (limousine). Lunch with Vera at Sherry Netherlands. **22** Business dinner at Oak Room with Natasha Nabokov. **25** Dr. Lewithin blood-take. **30** Influenza. **31** Bad day. Influenza. Dr. Lewithin. Dr. Lewithin *house call*.

1966

January

1 The Standard Diary for 1966: $2.00. At 5 p.m. Dick and George. **2** Dushkins, Edw. Allen, champagne, etc.

3 Prothrombin analysis. **5** At 8:30 to a musical comedy *Skyscraper* (with Julie Harris) (not for her!). Brilliant first act. Dances by Michael Kidd. Limousine. **6** For dinner at Totor [Vittorio] Rieti's. **7** Natasha Nabokov for dinner. **8** Natasha Nabokov at 2 for luncheon. George Balanchine at six for drinks. **9** Tape of "Variations" from Liebermann (Hamburg).[43] Customs $25.00. Elsie Rieti at 5. **10** Prothrombin analysis. 35% by nurse Victoria Pagan. **12** At Dr. Lewithin with Vera 1st venesection, 290 gr. Limousine. **13** Nabokov with his lady (dinner at the hotel). **14** At Dr. Lewithin, 2nd venesection, 270 gr. Limousine. **15** Lincoln Kirstein for lunch (here—hotel). At 5 my [CBS] film (television, D. Oppenheim). Limousine at 8 p.m. **16** Sam Dushkin at lunch. Party (dinner) at David Oppenheim house at 11 p.m. Limousine, Diagnostic Laboratory—blood-take prothrombin 38%. **17** Baldwin piano taken away. **18** Leaving New York for Minneapolis, Hotel Sheraton Ritz. **19** Rehearsal[44] *Fireworks* and *Baiser de la fée*. **20** Rehearsal. **21** Morning rehearsal. Concert at 8:30. After the concert, supper in the Grill Room of Sheraton Ritz Hotel with Lillian Libman and Elliott Carter. **22** Leaving Minneapolis at 2 p.m., arriving at Los Angeles. **25** Rehearsal at 10 a.m.[45] **26** Rehearsal at 10, rehearsal at 7 p.m. **27** Rehearsal at 10, 1st concert at 7. **28** 2nd concert. **30** The Montaperts at noon. At 5 p.m. Montapert and Andre. **31** Prothrombin time 34%.

February

1 Afternoon, flying to St. Louis,[46] Hotel Chase Park Plaza. Arriving St. Louis. **2** At 10 a.m., rehearsal. **3** Rehearsal at 10 a.m.; do not feel well: some temperature. **4** Antibiotics. Stay in. Did rehearsal at 8:30 p.m. *Capriccio* with Jocy De Oliveira and *Pulcinella* Suite. **5** Rehearsal at 10 a.m. Made my account with Lillian Libman. Commission for Los Angeles concert $500. Commission for St. Louis Concert $600. Concert in evening 8:30 p.m. **6** Matinée concert. Leaving St. Louis, arrived in Hollywood. **7** Milene in the afternoon. **9** At 8 p.m. Columbia recording of *Introitus*. **10** At 1:30 p.m. Columbia recording of *Cantata*: 1. Soprano aria. 2. A Lyke-Wake Dirge. Female chorus. Versus I, II, III, IV. **12** Vera received her driver's license. **13** Business dinner at Italian restaurant. **14** Prothrombin time 40%. **16** At 3 p.m., photographer. At 3:30 Milene to help me pack. **18** Flying to San Francisco to Hotel St. Francis. Dinner at the Hotel. **19** Rehearsal (orchestra) at 10 a.m. Dinner at Ernie's with Irina Arn. **20** Rehearsal (chorus). Dinner at Ernie's. **21** 3rd Concert at 8:30 p.m. **26** Leaving St. Francis Hotel. Arrival at Los Angeles.

March

3 Montaperts at 6:30 p.m. Drinks, appetizers. **4** Milene to help me for the baggage. **5** Prothrombin test 50%. Miranda. Dinner at Morton's. **6** Leaving Los Angeles to Rochester. Arriving at Rochester. **7** 1st rehearsal. **8** 2nd rehearsal. **9** 3rd rehearsal. **10** 4th rehearsal and 5th rehearsal.

---

[42] Stravinsky mentions her here only because she did *not* go to Washington.

[43] I made the recording in Hamburg in September 1965 with a microphone for each instrument in the 12-part variations. Stravinsky wanted the tape for Balanchine's guidance in choreographing the piece. (R.C.)

[44] Stravinsky has listed taxi fares for this and the second rehearsal even though he remained in bed reading Capote's *In Cold Blood*.

[45] Los Angeles Philharmonic: *St. Ann Fugue* (Bach-Schönberg), *Zvezdoliki*, *Symphony in C*, *Symphony of Psalms*.

[46] At the Los Angeles airport, the Stravinskys were shocked to read a newspaper story about the death of Anna Akhmatova. Mrs. Stravinsky did not make the trip, and the airplane carrying Stravinsky and myself was the last to land in snow-bound St. Louis. (R.C.)

11 Dress rehearsal. Concert at 8:30.   12 Leaving Rochester to NY. Arriving at NY in 50 minutes, Hotel Pierre. Mr. Paterson (London concert agent) for dinner here at the Pierre Hotel (business dinner).   13 Dr. Lewithin, hotel call at 11 a.m. Dinner: N. Nabokov.   14 To Dr. Lewithin with Vera. 1st venesection 325 gr.   15 To Dr. Lewithin with Vera. Vera to X-rays.   16 To Dr. Lewithin with Vera. 2nd venesection 250 gr.   17 Vera shopping for tomorrow's dinner with the Thomas Messers.   18 At 9:30 a.m., prothrombin test. At noon to Dr. Lewithin with Vera. 3rd venesection at noon. Arrival at Los Angeles, late, delay.   20 Dinner with Claudio Spies.   25 At 5 p.m., Mr. Harold Spivacke with wife. At 7 dinner with Marions.   27 Mrs. Arn (Honolulu Concert Agency) for dinner at home.

April

1 Moving: Sad news from Kitty. We sent Ampenova a cable asking to send Kitty immediately $1,000. Milene wrote her a letter.   4 Prothrombin test 37%. The pianists Babin and Vronsky. A small tea-party. Musical meeting, some projects. 6 Nikita Magaloff for luncheon.   9 Dinner with David Oppenheim.   11 Blood examination. Prothrombin 43.   13 For dinner, Mr. Magaloff (pianist) in connection with his performance tomorrow of my *Capriccio*—Philharmonic concert conducted by Mehta.   14 Sprezler at dinner (coming from Russia and performing new Russian music for me on tape).   18 Blood examination, prothrombin 55.   19 Dinner with Goddard Lieberson.   21 1st dinner party with Francis Steegmuller and Shirley Hazzard (*The Evening of the Holiday*), business party for Cocteau book.   22 2nd dinner party with F. Steegmuller and Shirley Hazzard, same as yesterday.   24 At 5:30 p.m. Montapert.   25 Blood examination, prothrombin 32%.   26 The singer (for recording).   30 Brigitta Zorina for dinner.

May

1 Brigitta Zorina for luncheon. Chez Isherwood and Don Bachardi, restaurant "Chianti."   3 Dinner Vera Zorina. 4 First bleeding Dr. Edel, 285 gr. Luncheon Brigitta Lieberson. Dinner Vera Zorina.   5 Carlos Chavez at dinner. Concert *Perséphone* with Zorina. After my concert, Miss Arn and a lot of people.   6 2nd bleeding (Edel) 250 gr.   7 Dentist (Dr. Charles Koplin). Dinner with Brigitta and Irina Arn. 8 Leaving Hollywood arriving N.Y. at 9 p.m., Pierre Hotel. 9 Prothrombin analysis. Third bleeding afternoon 275 gr. Dinner: E. Berman, Natasha.   10 E. Berman luncheon. I commissioned his drawings for *Rake's Progress* for $2,000. Ed. Allen. "Caravelle" with the Liebersons for dinner. Theater: Chekov's *Ivanov* (Gielgud).   11 4th bleeding (250 gr) blood pressure 140/85. Musical: "Sweet Charity." 12 Leaving N.Y. for Paris at 10 a.m. arrival Paris 10 p.m. Paris time. Met by Mario Bois, Lalandi, Dominique, Suvchinsky. Hôtel Lotti.   13 Lalandi (from Oxford) the whole day; contract.   14 Lalandi and Paterson. Vera to Balthus exposition [Louvre].   15 Lunch with Adriana Panni.   16 Dr. Pierre Thiroloix. Cramps . . . Brain trouble. Have to stay in bed. 17 Dr. Thiroloix.   18 Dr. Thiroloix.   19 Dr. Thiroloix.   20 Dr. Thiroloix with Professor Renée Marteau, neurologist.   21 Dr. Thiroloix.   22 Dr. Thiroloix. Afternoon: Vera with Bob in a car, secured by Mario Bois, to Meudon; Pierre Suvchinsky was my babysitter. Dinner at hotel with Bois and Suvchinsky.   23 Dr. Thiroloix at 9 a.m. Leaving Paris for

Athens at 3 p.m. Arrival at Athens to the Hilton Hotel. 24 2 rehearsals.   25 2 rehearsals.   26 Rehearsal and concert.   27 Leaving Athens, arrival at Lisbon, Hotel Ritz. 28 2 rehearsals.   30 2 rehearsals.   31 2 rehearsals.

June

1 Concert.   2 Leaving Lisbon, Hotel Ritz. Arriving at Paris, Hôtel Lotti.   3 Dr. Jacques Thiroloix (*frère*): blood pressure 167/70.   6 *Déjeuner avec Cartier-Bresson et ses amis.* At 5 p.m. to 10 p.m. Mario Bois.   7 Dr. Jacques Thiroloix. Dinner with Robert C., Pierre S., and both of us.   8 At Jacques Thiroloix.   9 At 10 a.m., nurse (pep!). At 5 p.m., Dr. Jacques Thiroloix. Afternoon Mr. Paterson (Diaghilev film [project]). At 7 p.m. Panni: *Soldat* with Manzù at Rome and Siracusa [project]. At 8 p.m. with Mr. and Mrs. Mario Bois to dinner. 10 Nurse. *Le soir avec les Bois au Restaurant en Ville d'Arrai. C'est Bois qui invite.*   11 Nurse. Dr. Jacques Thiroloix blood pressure 160/80, at 12 noon. Kitty at 12:30.   12 Nurse at 11 a.m. Bob and myself influenza. Dr. Pierre Thiroloix found in my left-side some bronchitis. Luxembourg and Strasburg concerts cancelled. Temp. 38.2. In the night 37.2, 36.6, 36.5. Perspiration. Rufina Ampenova came from London for a week.   13 Prothrombin test at 10. At 11, nurse with pep shot.   14 Pep shot nurse for last time. Dr. Pierre Thiroloix. 15 Dr. Pierre Thiroloix at 12 noon. Leaving with X-rays. 16 Dr. Thiroloix at 3 p.m.   17 Dr. Pierre Thiroloix during our lunch. Suvchinsky for dinner.   21 Leaving Paris Hôtel Lotti for New York, arrival at 2 p.m. (Lillian Libman). Baggage overweight $81.00!!! It was just the same as before when we didn't pay a cent. Pierre Hotel Dr. L. Lewithin house-call, myself and Bob.   22 9:20 a.m. Diagnostic Laboratory: urine, two bottles. 6 p.m. Dr. Lewithin.   23 Dr. Lewithin at 7 p.m. 24 Dr. Lewithin.   25 Lillian Libman for lunch. Dr. Lewithin at 1 p.m.   27 Dr. Lewithin at 5 p.m.   28 Same as 27th.   30 1st NY Philharmonic concert at 8:30 p.m. L. Bernstein *Sacre*.

July

1 Leaving NY, flight to Los Angeles.   7 Prothrombin test at 8:30 a.m. with Dr. Glass, Dr. Edel's substitute in his absence. Dr. Glass, with Suzanne (nurse), made a venesection 250 gr. 8 For luncheon S. Hurok and Miss L. Libman with Sarah, the caterer. I did not feel well. Semi-diarrhea. All kinds of usual medicines. Slept many hours. Very warm!   9 At 4:30 Mr. Grigorovich, Director of Bolshoi Ballet, Moscow. Bob took the train (airplane strike!) for Albuquerque-Santa Fe at 7 p.m. to conduct *The Rake's Progress* and *Wozzeck*.   11 Mr. Grigorovich, Director of Bolshoi Ballet for dinner.   12 6 p.m. Isherwood and Don Bachardi for drinks.   14 Left for NY at 10 a.m. flying at 11 a.m. American Airlines, all other airlines on strike. Arrival at NY at 6 p.m. NY time. Hotel Pierre.   15 To Lincoln Center to my concert (*Soldat*).   16 Lincoln Center Kondrashin. Russian program, *Petrushka*.   18 Lunch Lillian; we are going to the rehearsal of *The Flood*.   25 Leaving NY, Pierre Hotel, with Lillian Libman, arrival at Los Angeles airfield.   27 For lunch Miranda.   28 For lunch Miranda. 29 Our nice cook, Dagmar, deserted us with her son Pavil, too bad! For dinner Bill Brown.   31 Dinner with Montaperts at "La Rue."

August

1 Prothrombin test 8:30 a.m. Edel and his wife to dinner. 5 Dr. Edel house call. I have some temperature (throat) 38.4.

Antibiotics and antihistamin. **6** Temperature normal.
8 Prothrombin analysis at 8:30 a.m. **15** Prothrombin 45%.
18 For dinner Bill Brown. **19** Day of death of S. Diaghilev
(1929). For dinner: Chris. Isherwood, Don Bachardi, Miranda,
Morton. **22** Prothrombin test 45. **27** Lillian Libman away to
Mexico at 4 p.m. **28** 3rd time (cinema) "Khartoum," with Bob
and Morton. **29** Prothrombin 50. **30** Massage at 12:30 p.m.
by Dr. Hunt. **31** Massage Hunt.

September

1 Massage Hunt. **2** Massage Hunt. **3** Massage: Mr. Smith
11:30 a.m. **4** Massage. Smith 11:30 a.m. **5** Massage. Smith
10:30 a.m. **6** Massage 12:30 p.m. by Dr. Hunt. Prothrombin
test today 45%. At Edel, venesection at 10:30. **7** Massage
Hunt. For dinner, Bill Brown and Morton. **8** Massage Hunt.
Temperature 38. Bad night. All day in bed. **9** Massage Hunt
at 11:30 a.m. At dinner business people. Montapert.
10 Massage Smith. **11** Massage Smith. **12** Massage Hunt.
Prothrombin test 42%. Lillian Libman back from Mexico.
13 Massage Hunt. Venesection 250 gr. Dr. Edel. **14** Flying
early in the morning to Louisville. **17** Concert in Louisville:
Fireworks (I), *Sacre* (Bob), *Firebird Suite* (I). **18** Leaving
Louisville for NY. Plane in the afternoon. **20** Prothrombin
test. **21** 1st venesection Dr. Lewithin 275 gr. **23** 2nd
venesection Dr. Lewithin 250 gr. Taxi with Vera $5.00.
24 Prothrombin test. **27** 3rd venesection Dr. Lewithin at high
300 gr. **28** At Dr. S. La Due (34 E. 67): consultation with Dr.
L. Lewithin. **29** At 11:30 a.m. at Dr. Harold Temple (50 E 70).
Röntgen X-rays. **30** Vera's Name Day. Lunch with
Liebersons at CBS. Theatre with McClures (supper at
L'Étoile).

October

1 Lunch with Bill Brown and Cl. Spies at 5 p.m. Arnold
Newman—photos! photos! photos! **2** For dinner Edw. Allen,
Jean vanden Heuvel, Bob. **3** At 2 p.m. Dr. Harold Temple.
Rehearsal 2:30 to 6:30. At 6 p.m. Dr. Lewithin and Dr. La
Due. **4** Rehearsal. **5** Rehearsal at 2 p.m. **6** Grand
rehearsal from 1 to 7 p.m. Bar: Dinner with Lawrence Morton,
Claudio Spies, Edw. Allen, Watkins. **7** Luncheon with Jean
vanden Heuvel. **8** Limousine. Luncheon. Rehearsal.
Princeton Concert at 8:30. Premiere *Requiem Canticles*.
Limousine to Hotel Pierre. **10** At 6 p.m. Dr. Lewithin and Dr.
La Due: digitalis at 7:30, 1 tablet, 8:30 1 tablet, 9:30 1 tablet.
11 At 11 a.m. a new X-ray of my chest at Dr. Harold Temple.
At Dr. Lewithin venesection 300 gr. After breakfast digitalis 1
tablet. Visit from Sir Is. Berlin. Digitalis 2nd tablet. Recording
4 to 11 p.m. **12** Leaving NY for Hollywood. We arrived at
5:30; Milene met us. Our cook—sick (drunk!—Vera did the
dinner). **13** I am sick (flu). **14** Twenty-five years of our
church wedding here in Los Angeles in the big church.
Lawrence Morton for dinner. **17** At 5:45 the Montaperts. He
took the Princeton letter of the University President asking
me to give to the University the manuscript of my *Requiem
Canticles*. He will answer to him and bring me a copy of his
approval. I decided to *give* it to them. **19** Dinner at Morton.
2 bottles of champagne. **20** Soulima came in the morning.
Dinner with him at the Marions. Bob's birthday. **21** Dinner
with Soulima and Marions here at home. Sarah. **22** Soulima

went away at 9 a.m. **24** At 8 a.m., prothrombin test 48%.
25 Bernal[47] and Bob working for my film. Dinner at "La
Scala." **26** Vera at eye Dr. Dow. **28** Photographer Newman
every day. **29** Photographer Newman every day.
30 Evening rehearsal of my *Owl and Pussy-Cat*.
31 Photographer Newman went away.

November

2 Restaurant "Chasens," bad and expensive. Photographer
Newman back. **3** Dr. Edel, Vera. **4** Vera all day in her bed.
Cardiogram Dr. Edel. Limousine. At 1 p.m. to Pasadena. 1st
rehearsal *Dumbarton Oaks*, 1st and 3rd parts. **5** At 2 p.m.
Pasadena rehearsal: *Pulcinella* (myself) Beethoven *Symphony*
(R. Craft). **6** Rehearsal—Marions, Montaperts. I. Arn for
drinks. **7** At 8:30 p.m., concert. **12** Leaving Los Angeles to
Honolulu at 11:30, 5-hour flight arriving at 7 p.m. [sic] Hawaii
time. Kahala Hilton Hotel. Dinner at the hotel with Irina Arn
and the Montaperts. **13** Dinner at the hotel, downstairs, Irina
Arn, the Montaperts. **14** Rehearsal, evening. **15** Rehearsal,
evening. **16** Dinner Montaperts' invitation. **17** Rehearsal,
evening. **18** Party (orchestra). I am drunk! **19** Rehearsal
(evening). **20** Morning rehearsal. Concert at 4 p.m.
21 *Mutations*, series. Dinner outside Honolulu. **22** Concert
(evening). **23** Leaving Honolulu for Hollywood. Arriving Los
Angeles. Home for 48 hours. Big dinner. Marions, Jack Quinn,
Marilyn Stalvey. **24** Thanksgiving Day. Dinner at Milene.
25 Leaving home to Columbus, Ohio, Hilton Hotel.
26 Rehearsal. **28** 2 rehearsals. **29** Rehearsal. Concert in
Veterans Memorial Auditorium at 8:30 p.m. **30** University:
Bob's lecture. *Histoire du soldat*. Leaving Columbus, Ohio, to
Chicago. Arriving Chicago. Eating at the airfield. Leaving
Chicago to Portland Hilton Hotel.

December

1 2 rehearsals. **2** Dinner with Irina Arn and 2 friends of R.
Craft: Mark DeVoto and his pregnant wife. Rehearsal. **3** No
rehearsals. Dinner with Anita Lourié. My plastic cane
broken!!! Cannot walk!!!!!! **6** 2nd concert in Portland. **7** Back
home! From Hilton Portland to Hollywood. **8** Letter to Nadia
(Paris) and cable. At 5 p.m. *beautiful film* (yet without my
music).[48] At 7:30 a.m. Lillian Libman came to stay a few days
at our home. **9** Laboratory: prothrombin test. 10 years of my
thrombosis when Munich Prof. Dr. Diehl took me for weeks to
his hospital. Lunch with many people. Bob's film with my
music, here at home. Evening "Chianti Restaurant" with
Lillian Libman. Supper at "Pavilion" (Music Center).
12 Bleeding nose. Dr. Edel, Arnold Newman photos for
album. **13** Party: E. Evtushenko, his secretary. Photographer
6:30. Dinner at 8. **14** Dr. Edel, Vera, Bob. Film: United Air
Lines. **15** Recording for United Air Lines. **16** Dinner Dr.
Edel at "Chasens," L. Libman, A. Newman, 2 Edels,
Stravinskys, Bob Craft. **17** "Pavilion" dinner Lillian Libman
invitation. **18** Marions back from Cambria. Dinner. Vera
went to Miranda's party. Arnold Newman: Photos! photos!
19 Schütz's *Christmas Oratorio* in the Los Angeles County
Museum. Big dinner at "Luau." **20** S. Hurok. Lunch with him
at "Bistro." **21** Dr. Edel, Vera. Montapert. Tax examination.
22 Packing, packing, packing. **23** Morning, Dr. Edel. Vera at
1 p.m., flying to Chicago Hotel Drake. **24** Vera's birthday—

---

[47] Bill Bernal was the script-writer for a United Air Lines publicity film using Stravinsky's music. Bernal stayed in the Stravinsky home.

[48] The United Air Lines travelog.

Mink coat! Theatre at 8:30 "The Odd Couple." Limousine. Dinner at "Maxim's" [Harry] Zelzer invitation. Limousine. **27** Morning rehearsal. **28** Rehearsal. Soulima arrival. Evening concert. Limousine. Supper (7 persons) at the Drake Hotel. **29** Lunch with Soulima in the hotel. Dinner party (Clyde Krebs). **30** Lunch with Glenn Watkins. Dinner. Glenn Watkins invitation.

1968

February

10 Our trip (airplane) to San Francisco (St. Francis Hotel) for my three symphony concerts. Concerts in Oakland (California) under the direction of Robert Craft—my supervision. **13** 1st concert in Oakland. **14** 2nd concert in Oakland. **15** 3rd concert in Oakland.

April

23 Asked Bob to compose opera libretto for me. He agreed.

When the Stravinskys flew from Los Angeles to New York in September 1968, the composer carried a statement from his hematologist, Irwin M. Weinstein, certifying that "Mr Stravinsky has Polycythemia Rubra Vera"—which had been the diagnosis, in October 1967, of another Beverly Hills doctor, J. Pincus, who, however, had added the ominous words, "out of control." Stravinsky was first examined by Dr. Weinstein on April 4, 1968. His report on that occasion was that Stravinsky "complained of severe pruritis" and of a "sensation that his eyes are pulling in different directions, particularly when he looks downward." Weinstein found no "evidence of purpura or icterus" but he mentioned that "the spleen was not palpable, the liver was palpable at the right costal margin." On this date the red blood cell count was 5,000,000, the "massively increased" platelet count, 1,074,000. Prothrombin consumption was 26 seconds in an hour. The document also states that Stravinsky "has not received radioactive phosphorus in six months," though in fact this treatment had been stopped five years before that.

Weinstein's reports of April 17, April 24, and May 8, 1968, record remarkable improvements, the platelet count, for one, having fallen to 494,000. On May 9, Weinstein permitted his illustrious patient to fly to San Francisco to attend a festival in his honor at Berkeley, though during the period Stravinsky required daily injections of Heparin against arterio-embolization (administered by Dr. Ralph Wallerstein).

In New York, Stravinsky immediately called on Dr. Leon Lewithin, his physician for the preceding six years. A blood analysis, September 17, revealed a platelet count of 210,000 and a hematocrit rate of 52%. The red blood cells showed anisocytosis and poikilocytosis, but this had been noted some years before. Stravinsky's doctor in Zürich, Max Probst, a general practitioner, ordered hematological examinations performed on the composer six times in two weeks (twice on September 30, 1968, once on October 9, once on October 10, and twice on October 15), with good results, a low platelet count and a fluctuation of the hematocrit between 44% and 53%.

In Paris, on October 24, Stravinsky had an electro-radiological examination by Dr. André Chateau, and on the 28th a complete hematological analysis under the care of Dr. Thiroloix, in which the platelets were down to 118,000. In November, Stravinsky returned to California and to Dr. Weinstein, the most successful of all the composer's hematologists. In June–August 1970, Stravinsky was again in France, under the care of Dr. R. Della Santa of Geneva, who favored phlebotomy, and under whose supervision Stravinsky was bled several times in Thonon-les-Bains. Back in New York, and for the remaining seven-and-a-half months of his life, Stravinsky received no hematological treatment, nor, apparently, did he suffer any more from polycythemia.